Praise For

*More Than Your Mindset*

"*More Than Your Mindset* encourages readers to examine their mindsets and go on a personal journey of growth. Karen shares about herself in a vulnerable and authentic way so we can relate to her and understand how to apply the lessons provided. After reading this book you will be challenged to be a better version of yourself."

—Alan Werner, Vice President of Sales, Real Colors

"This is a powerful exploration of the inner workings of our thinking and its impact. This book is funny, charming, inspiring, loving, and immensely healing. Karen does an amazing job opening up about her own foibles and failings in her journey, and an even better job sharing how those lessons have made her stronger, more effective, and more able to serve the world around her. She walks us through patterns in our thinking that guide us in positive ways. She provides interactive tools and a set of guidelines that can impact relationships, careers, family, and more."

—Dr. Jennifer Murphy, DEL Author,
*The Art of Living Dangerously*:
*The rebels guide to thriving in a world that expects you to conform*

"This book is like attending one of Karen's workshops, from the comfort of your sofa or while relaxing at the beach. She combines real stories with prompts to understand yourself and a thoughtful guide on how to live a more mindful, purposeful, and rewarding life."

—Patti M. Seda, Executive Coach and Author,
*Discovering Job Joy, Your Guide to Stretching Without Snapping*

# MORE THAN YOUR MINDSET

## HOW TO LIVE A MORE POSITIVE AND ENERGIZED LIFE

Karen Schumacher

More Than Your Mindset How to Live a More Positive and Energized Life
Copyright © 2021 by Karen Schumacher.

All rights reserved. No part of this publication may be reproduced, distributed, or transmitted in any form or by any means, including photocopying, recording, or other electronic or mechanical methods, without the prior written permission of the author, except in the case of brief quotations embodied in critical reviews and certain other noncommercial uses permitted by copyright law.

Disclaimer:

The author strives to be as accurate and complete as possible in the creation of this book, notwithstanding the fact that the author does not warrant or represent at any time that the contents within are accurate due to the rapidly changing nature of the Internet.

While all attempts have been made to verify information provided in this publication, the Author and the Publisher assume no responsibility and are not liable for errors, omissions, or contrary interpretation of the subject matter herein. The Author and Publisher hereby disclaim any liability, loss or damage incurred as a result of the application and utilization, whether directly or indirectly, of any information, suggestion, advice, or procedure in this book. The author tried to recreate events, locales and conversations from her memories of them. In order to maintain their anonymity in some instances the names of individuals, places, dates, and some identifying details or characteristics may have been changed.

Photographs courtesy of Pixabay, The Illusion Index, and Shutterstock.

Thomson, G. and Macpherson, F. (June 2018), "Scintillating Grid" in F. Macpherson (ed.), The Illusions Index. Retrieved from https://www.illusionsindex.org/i/scintillating-grid.

Printed in the United States of America

ISBN: 978-1-948382-28-1 paperback
JMP2021.5

This book is dedicated to my mom and dad for shaping me, encouraging me, and loving me through the good times and the bad; to my brothers and sister who challenge me, protect me, and accept me as me; to my husband who inspires me, pushes me to be my best self, supports me in hard times and not only the easy ones, and believes in me even when I am doubtful of myself; and of course, for my children, Ashlee, Morgan, and Kyle, for making me laugh, making me cry (in a good way), and making me better.

To the countless others who have come and gone or are still in my life. Those who were there on purpose and by chance. Most importantly, I give thanks to God.

# Contents

| | |
|---|---:|
| Introduction | 1 |
| Chapter 1: Formulate Your Thoughts | 7 |
|    A Picture Doesn't Tell the Entire Story | 8 |
|    Changing Your Thinking | 16 |
|    What You Look For Is What You Will Find | 22 |
|    Don't Judge Others … | 28 |
|    Understanding Mindset and Self-Talk | 40 |
|    Tell Yourself a Different Story | 42 |
|    There Once Was a Time for Me to Sing | 47 |
|    In Summary: Formulate Your Thoughts | 48 |
|    Turn Your Learning into Action | 50 |
| Chapter 2: Reinvent You | 53 |
|    Identifying Your Core Values | 70 |
|    Exploring Your Core Values | 81 |
|    Understanding Your Personal Brand | 82 |
|    Creating Your Vision | 85 |
|    Turning Your Vision into Reality | 88 |
|    In Summary: Reinvent You | 102 |
|    Turn Your Learning into Action | 104 |

- Chapter 3: Engage with Others .......... 105
  - When the Impossible Happens .......... 105
  - The Baby Porcupines .......... 108
  - Build Authentic Relationships .......... 114
  - Being Vulnerable and Transparent .......... 124
  - Getting Others to Get Along with You .......... 133
  - Engage on the Level of the Person .......... 137
  - In Summary: Engage with Others .......... 138
  - Turn Your Learning into Action .......... 140
- Chapter 4: Energize Yourself .......... 143
  - My Tips for Stress Management and Positive Energy .......... 153
  - Seven Types of People to Be Around .......... 162
  - Don't Hold Mistakes against Others or Yourself .......... 166
  - In Summary: Energize Yourself .......... 168
  - Turn Your Learning into Action .......... 169
- Conclusion .......... 171
  - PEZ Dispensers .......... 173
  - Sing Your Song .......... 174
- About the Author .......... 177

# Introduction

Before we go any further, you need to know—I *love* to sing. Singing makes me *happy*. If I could have done anything different with my life, I would have been a professional singer. When I listen to music and sing along, I'm transformed to another place. I feel different. I'm more motivated. I'm in my happy place. When my brother Jim, who is twenty-months younger, and I were children we would sing for our parents and grandparents. We did rounds of "Frère Jacques," "Row, Row, Row Your Boat," and songs we learned in Sunday school. We were quite the performers, even adding in dance moves. We were the next "Donny and Marie" for a moment in time. I remember on one visit to my great-grandmother and a couple great-aunts in a nursing home in California, our Dad encouraged us to sing for everyone. We received lots of applause. I was so happy making others happy doing what made me happy. But the truth is . . . I can't sing. I'm so bad at singing. I try. I *really* do . . . but even my own children will tell me in church, as I bellow out to my favorite praise songs, that they're sure God is happy and pleased, but those around us should not be subjected to that sound. Wow.

Truth. It's what we believe, whether it's right or wrong. Sometimes, we're faced with truth and choose to ignore it. We don't want to believe it because we think it can't possibly be . . . true. Our truth is what we tell ourselves about ourselves, about others, about situations. We don't just tell ourselves; we choose to believe it, even when we're wrong. It's easy to make up a story in our mind and convince ourselves that is the *truth*. The *only* truth. For some of us, once we get there, it's hard to get out. I often think about why I was so confident to sing when I was a child and can't now as an adult. I thought I sounded good, others told me I sounded good, it seemed to make others happy, it made me happy—therefore, I must be a good singer. Maybe. Things change. I didn't train to sing. I don't have natural talent. I sound different as an adult than I did as child. I've even tried to barter with God. If He gave me the ability to sing well, I would only sing praise songs. But, alas, I'll have to wait for that day when I'm able to sing in heaven. Until that day, I'll sing in my car—alone—as loudly as I want and feel good without causing anyone else any ear pain . . . unless you pull up next to my vehicle, even when my windows are up.

In our minds we store our truth and live it out. When I become really stressed is when my mindset shifts to victim thinking or as I call it, the "woe is me" syndrome. Have you ever found yourself in a funk and had to pull yourself out of it? Perhaps you're stuck in a job you don't like but convinced yourself there isn't anything better. Maybe, you keep getting overlooked for a new position or you don't even apply for it because it's easier to tell yourself you wouldn't get it or that you aren't qualified rather than face rejection. Do you struggle with certain relationships in your professional or personal life because you think they don't like you or you've decided you don't like them? For some people, they are true victims of a situation or circumstance but allow that situation or circumstance to define them. Maybe like me, you aren't good at something, but you dwell on that one thing and put yourself down because of it. We all have been there. We all have good days and bad days. It's hard though, especially when bad days seem to outnumber our good days, making it easier to jump to conclusions, to shift blame, and to have a negative outlook. I found in my life, both personally and professionally, I've the perfect recipe for negative thinking: create thoughts about a person, situation, or yourself; sprinkle it with examples of why you're right; add a dash of other people's perspectives, especially those who agree with you; and, presto, you have created a mindset so strong it's hard for you or anyone else to change it.

This book is about how to learn how to change our mindsets for a more positive outlook. How to find a better story we can tell ourselves so that we can do things differently and have better results and live a more positive and energized life. When I think about past situations that weren't the outcome I wanted, I think about how I may have come across to others by what I said or didn't say and how I acted or reacted.

I've been giving presentations and workshops on changing mindsets and how to live more positively since the early 2000s. This book is for anyone who wants to be more aware of their own mindset and behaviors, for those who want to grow and be better and even for those who don't know they need to grow and be more self-aware. This book has many stories of things I've done well and things I didn't do well. I hope they help you grow as much as I grew from these experiences.

My hope is that this book will provoke positive change in how you think, act, respond, and engage with others. I'm not a psychologist. I don't have a PhD. I'm a Christian woman: a mom, wife, sister, daughter, aunt, cousin, niece. I'm a good friend to some and need to be a better friend to others. I'm awkward. I don't always fit in. Sometimes I'm right and sometimes I get it all wrong. I'm a people-pleaser, a loner, a big-picture thinker, a crier, a rule-follower (most of the time, but not always). I like to research things that I find interesting. I don't like to be wrong. I like to compete, but not willing to win if there's more that I could lose. I'm an executive coach, a business owner, a corporate trainer, a motivational speaker, a storyteller (I get that from my dad). I love to tell jokes (I get this from my dad too). I'm a volunteer, a giver, a life-long learner (I get these from my mom). I get frustrated with bad drivers, long lines, and people who are cruel to others. I'm enthusiastic, full of energy, and a big-idea person. I can be shy. There are times when I'm filled with self-doubt. Like many others, there are times I struggle with anxiety and depression. I've been told that I forgive too easily (I forgive because I've been forgiven). Although, I've been known to hold a grudge and taken longer to forgive a few people. I'm not perfect. I'm not in a place to judge others. I'm me. I'm qualified to write this book because I've been living this for most of my life. I'm an ordinary person trying to live life, trying to survive, trying to make a difference. That's it.

I've been told that I'm too positive for some people and that if I had experienced the "bad" things other people have, then maybe I would have a more realistic disposition. For me, being positive is a choice and something I work at each day. While I may not have the exact same experiences as others, I have had my share of good and bad things happen in my life. In this book I share stories that may make you laugh and cry. These are the personal successes and tragedies that challenged my mindset, made my faith stronger, and allowed me to learn to be a victor, not a victim to my circumstances.

My intent was to make this book an interactive session between you and yourself. I share personal stories from my life with the hope they help make a point, create a visual, and evoke emotion. (People, situations, and some details have been changed to protect their anonymity.) This book is based on my experiences, on what I've learned and how I try to live. I hope it will give you a chance to self-evaluate as you explore your outlook and personal brand. This is your book so make it yours. Be honest with yourself as you think and answer different questions and work through exercises.

The goal is to learn to live a more positive and energized life. While there will always be some type of negativity in our lives, we can focus on what we can do to reduce negativity in us and around us. This book uses the acronym FREE to give you ideas how to

**Formulate your thoughts:** Apply tips and techniques for more positive thinking.

**Reinvent you:** Decide what changes you need to make to your personal brand based on your words, behaviors, and attitude.

**Engage with others:** Identify how you motivate or demotivate others and how to better connect with people—especially those with different personality styles.

**Energize yourself:** Utilize strategies to energize yourself through the day.

## 💡 Personal Activity: Explore why you're reading this book.

**Start with answering these questions:**

What is my goal in reading and working through this book?

Look at your answer. Why is this important to you?

Look at your answer. Why is this important to you?

Look at your answer. Why is this important to you?

Look at your answer. Why is this important to you?

Look at your answer. Why is this important to you?

Your last answer (your fifth why) is likely your true reason for reading this book. Remember, be honest with yourself as you work through these exercises.

# CHAPTER 1:
# FORMULATE YOUR THOUGHTS

My freshman year of high school, I made the debate team. I'd like to say I made the team as if I had beat out others, but I actually *made* the debate team because if I hadn't gone out, we wouldn't have had enough students to form a team ... in which there were four of us. Our subject for the entire school year was capital punishment. Our team was prepared to argue for or against it. We didn't know which argument we would have to give and defend until we were at the meet. By the end of the season, I could argue both sides so well that even to this day I can confuse any person who has a strong stance one way or another. I even confuse myself and change my mind on what I believe about capital punishment.

One of my favorite quotes I see around the internet is: "When you change the way you look at things, the things you look at change." This quote is so true, especially for me. When I train and coach on conflict resolution, I often do an exercise, like being on a debate team, where I have the parties argue from the other person's point of view. This forces them to look at things differently. Sometimes when taking a different look at a subject or situation it may change a person's mind. Sometimes when the other party hears someone else arguing their point, they may hear it differently and change their mind. You may have heard there are three sides to the truth: my side, your side, and the actual truth somewhere in the middle. It's important to get all the details, facts, information, and perspectives and understand your emotions before making a statement or taking a hard stance that you alienate others or create a negative reputation for yourself.

## A Picture Doesn't Tell the Entire Story

As you look at this picture, what do you see?

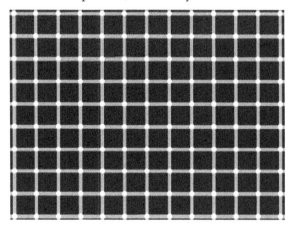

It appears to be changing right before your eyes—even on this paper! That is the one thing we can be certain about: change is constant. We're always changing and evolving. We change our minds; we change our stance on issues; we change our looks; we change our friends and who we associate with; we change jobs or careers; we change what we eat or drink; we change where we grocery shop; we change where we live; we change where we vacation—we change. That's part of life and it's necessary for us to continue to grow and be better. Sometimes we choose these changes and sometimes changes are thrust on us.

Chapter 1: Formulate Your Thoughts

Now look at these pictures:

What do you see when you look at these pictures?

How do you feel when you look at them?

The most common answers I get are "Looks like real life" and "Just another day in our world" and "Doesn't look like good news." Some say they can see hope, others see anxiety. Some see joy, others see depression. No matter what you see, you're correct. What we see in these pictures may not be the entire story. It depends on you and on how you interpret them. It depends on where you are and what you have going on around you in life—at home, at work, with others. A story is perceived in your mind based on how you feel in the moment. If you're happy and content with things in life in the moment, such as your job, career, family, relationships, friends, faith, life, then you might see the more positive attributes of these pictures. If you're frustrated, angry, bitter, defeated, then you might see the more negative aspects of these pictures. Is the glass half empty or half full? The answer, by the way, is *yes*.

We're busy people. Some have families, jobs, school; we have bills to pay, mouths to feed, homework to do, jobs to work, or other expectations. Likely, we all have some forms of responsibilities. It's easy for us to view a person or situation and make stuff up about that person or situation based on our belief system. This is how we make sense of the world.

Your belief system is based on your experiences. Where did you grow up—in a small town, on a farm, or in a big city? What type of family did you have—large or small; close-knit or distant; were you the oldest, youngest, middle, or only child? Did you have a blended family? A broken family? Were your parents married, divorced, remarried, never married? Did you belong to a sports team, play a musical instrument, act in a play, sit on student council, or participate in a different school club or not do any extracurricular activities? Did you enjoy school or dislike it? Did you have more positive experiences and people or more negative experiences and people in your life?

It's based on your personal history. Generations are shaped by the experiences they had in their teenage years, such as world events, fads, music, and moments. I believe we're shaped by both good events in our lives *and* through any suffering and tribulations we've faced. Put all these together and you have how you view the world and life. We become conditioned for what we expect of ourselves, others, and situations. We create narratives and give meaning to the things we experience—good and bad.

Do you watch the news before you go to bed? Majority of people when asked in my workshops say they don't. When I ask why, I'm told because it's depressing. The main stories are focused on the "bad news" happening in our communities, in our state, or in the world. The headlines aren't "BREAKING NEWS: a report just in, a new company is coming to our community and bringing 250 new jobs" . . . or a cure for cancer has been reported and already saved thousands of lives . . . or an anonymous person made a huge donation for a new homeless shelter. Unfortunately, the main stories are of another company downsizing or closing their doors, another day where stocks fall, another CEO caught embezzling money, another mass shooting, another child missing, another sexual harassment case, a pandemic bringing our health system to its knees and close to financial brink. While those are reality, there's good news also. Sometimes it might be the first story, the last story, or buried in the middle, but they're there. I surveyed 100 people in 2019 about the news of the day. Here is what I found:

- 7% could share a positive story they heard.
- 48% could tell me the main stories happening worldwide.

- 76% knew stories happening locally.
- 3% didn't care either way.
- 65% didn't watch the news before they went to bed.
- 33% didn't watch the news before they went to bed but did start their day with it.

Here is the interesting part: when asked to tell me what they could remember, they said it with dismay. No one was excited and full of joy.

I took my experiment a little further and engaged in conversations with 100 strangers. I asked them questions and listened to them about themselves, if they liked what they did or if they told me about their children or grandchildren—most smiled and were happy to talk. However, when I asked about a topic that was relevant in the news, they changed. I could see their emotional state change. Some people grew angry at the situations, others got sad or depressed, yet others didn't show any emotion, almost as if they're full of apathy toward the situation. I switched the topic back to the one that brought them happiness and they shifted with me (I thought it was better to leave them in a positive mood).

## ☀ Personal Activity: What's your truth?

For each of the following that apply to you, decide when you have more of a negative or positive view. Then note why you have that viewpoint *most* of the time.

Your job, company, or school:

1. Is your view more negative or positive *most* of the time? Why?

2. When do you have more of a negative view?

3. When do you have more of a positive view?

Your boss or teacher/professor:

1. Is your view more negative or positive *most* of the time? Why?

2. When do you have more of a negative view?

3. When do you have more of a positive view?

Your peers or friends:

1. Is your view more negative or positive *most* of the time? Why?

2. When do you have more of a negative view?

3. When do you have more of a positive view?

Your city or neighborhood:

1. Is your view more negative or positive *most* of the time? Why?

2. When do you have more of a negative view?

3. When do you have more of a positive view?

Your church, pastor/priest, faith or God:

1. Is your view more negative or positive *most* of the time? Why?

2. When do you have more of a negative view?

3. When do you have more of a positive view?

Your family members (i.e., parent, spouse, child(ren), sibling, etc.):

1. Is your view more negative or positive *most* of the time? Why?

2. When do you have more of a negative view?

3. When do you have more of a positive view?

## Changing Your Thinking

In 2008, I was leading a training department for a local company. A manager in the company came to me with a flier for a motivational seminar coming to our city. There was special pricing that read something like "Send your entire office for one low price of $9.99." I also received that flyer but dismissed it because my mindset was it was a scam. Other managers started asking me about it, so I decided to call and find out. To my surprise, I not only spoke to a very cheerful and helpful young woman but was reassured by her that that special was indeed accurate. Again, with hesitation I verified, "So, if I'm hearing you correctly, I can send five-hundred people and only have to pay $9.99 one-time?" She said yes. I told her not to worry because we couldn't send everyone together for a full-day seminar. I could almost feel her smiling.

As it turned out we had about twenty people, including myself, who were able to attend. I preordered our workbooks at a discounted rate, and an additional five workbooks because a few others couldn't attend but still wanted the materials. Here we go! The day of the seminar we met at our local convention center downtown. While waiting for the rest of the team to arrive, I got our workbooks. Remember, I preordered a total of twenty-five workbooks. After getting the stack back and counting them, I realized I had one too many. As I tried to give it back to the person helping us, he said, "It's okay, you can keep it. We have so many that it won't matter." Really? I get to keep it? That is AWESOME because one more person wanted a copy of the workbook and I was going to give them mine and now I don't have to. I thanked the gentleman and told him that he made my day. He simply smiled and said he was glad to help.

As we entered the convention center, we found enough seats for our group to be together in a couple rows. Now, I'm not a control freak . . . all the time. Someone else in our group had the workbooks, and upon sitting down, they put them on a chair that separated us from . . . strangers. I didn't like that. I was consumed with thinking that someone was going to take our workbooks. You need to understand that I grew up in South Side, Chicago. That was my reality. People took things that weren't theirs, often. If we left our bikes or roller skates out overnight, they likely were gone by morning. One morning we left the house to see someone stole the battery out of our Dad's car. That happened several times over the years. Our house had been broken into, twice. It only made sense to me that these workbooks would be taken if not properly watched.

Finally, the lights go down and people were on the stage shouting with excitement, "Are you ready to get motivated?" The crowd stood and cheered. My heart raced as the energy was so powerful. After having us sit down and going through the introductions and expectations of the day, it was now time for the first speaker. They asked us to open our workbooks. After we passed ours out to our attendees, I ask for the extras to be given to me (to satisfy that control thing). When the extras got to me, I was expecting six but only five came. I knew it! I knew someone was going to take a workbook. Okay, now I need to change my mindset. What did my mom always tell me? If someone took something of yours, they must have needed it more than you. Only one was taken and we didn't pay for that workbook. I was feeling better and now able to concentrate.

That morning Zig Ziglar came on stage. He said something so profound that made a lot of sense to me. He said, "If you have stinking thinking going on, then you need a check-up from the neck up." As he went on, he talked about how we need to program our thoughts from negative to positive. This wasn't new to me. I had been training on positive thinking and the concept of *you get what you give* for decades. For some reason that day, I needed to hear it instead of training it. That message was meant for me. Soon it was time for a break. As we piled out to stretch and walk around, I noticed on the floor under the chair that originally held our twenty-six workbooks was that one lonely workbook I thought was stolen. It simply had fallen to the ground. It hit me. I had stinking thinking and needed a check-up from the neck up. I was so convinced of my past being the only truth—that nothing else could have been a reason for that missing workbook. I'm a pretty positive person. What I discovered that day was that I had some deep-rooted truths that I hadn't explored from a different point of view, and that maybe I wasn't as positive as I thought I was.

Change your thinking. That was the biggest learning I got from that seminar. A different outcome starts with what I think about someone or something. This made me think about what other things I believe to be true that maybe weren't. For instance, what I thought about myself, friends, my job, coworkers. I remembered back to my freshman year in high school. I had gone to a Lutheran elementary school from fourth grade until eighth grade. For high school though, we went to a Chicago public high school. I was pretty sheltered from *real* life. Other than people stealing from us, I hadn't experienced yet what high school gave me only three weeks into the new school year. To help with the transition and because it was my birthday, my mom bought me a new outfit. This was in the early 1980s. Normally we shopped at the Sears Outlet store. We had the dark-blue, stiff jeans. We didn't have designer clothes. If I did have anything with a designer name, it was because of the hand-me-downs I got from friends or cousins or because we bought them ourselves with our own earned money. This new outfit was a yellow jumper with a black T-shirt. It was exactly what was in style. I couldn't wait to wear it to school. I wanted to fit in. I wanted to look good. I had graduated eighth grade with twelve other students. We were all good friends. We didn't care about what each other wore or how we looked. But now I was going to high school and didn't know anyone.

My freshman class had 923 students. There were over 4,000 students in the school. That's bigger than some small towns! I only wanted to fit in, not stand out. I was awkward and shy and thought this new outfit will help me. On the day I wore it to school, hours into the day I was stopped in the girl's bathroom. Six girls surrounded me. One had a knife. They started talking to me in Spanish. I didn't understand them or what was happening. I started to cry. Finally, one of them said, "Oh, let her go. She's not a gang member. She's just a stupid little girl." Wait—what? Gangs? Like in *West Side Story* gangs? (I grew up going to musicals; that's what I could relate to . . .) "Excuse me . . . um . . . why did you think I was a gang member?" I cautiously asked. The leader of the group said, "Honey, don't know you know?" I wasn't sure if she wanted me to actually answer that as the answer was *no* because if I knew I wouldn't be doing whatever it is that I was doing to make anyone believe I was in a gang. (A bit of trivia—I wouldn't learn this until after my grandfather passed away and not for many years after this situation—he was part of Al Capone's "gang" during the prohibition.) I was smart enough not to smart off. She went on to tell me the color combination of yellow and black were the rival colors of that part of the city's gangs. Needless to say, I didn't wear that outfit to school again, or at least not with the same t-shirt.

My belief system at that time shifted to *everyone at a Chicago public high school must be dangerous.* I learned, over time, that wasn't true. I made some great friends at that school. The following year I went to a different high school. Still Chicago but out of my district. It wasn't because of gangs, either. Remember how I can't sing? My first high school was a performing arts school, and I didn't have the talent to sing, dance, or play music. (Although I've played the song flute, clarinet, piano, organ, and, thanks to my dad, the accordion—his accordion. That's a different story for another time.) So, I transferred to a computer-technical high school and made new friends.

By the way: who knew in my life's journey I would move to a city and state where almost everyone wears yellow and black because of the Iowa Hawkeyes, unless you're an Iowa State or University of Northern Iowa student, alumni, family, or fan. The overwhelming amount of yellow and black would make you think they're their own gang. (And really, with their loyalty, they kind of are. I believe my stepdaughter's mom, Paulette, is the leader of the Hawkeye gang because she is their biggest fan I know!)

Starting over my sophomore year was like freshman year. I wasn't supposed to be the new kid, again. I was supposed to have a set group of friends, people to eat with, someone to talk to, a place where I fit in. It was bad enough my freshman year that I asked seven guys—yes, seven—to go to homecoming with me. I wound up going with my cousin. I already struggled with my perception of myself. Now I had to try again to fit in. My sophomore year I only asked three guys to go with me, and after they all said no, I just didn't go. I even made a card from scratch with Snoopy on it asking an upperclassman to go. He was at least sweet on how he told me no.

I already confessed that I was awkward and how I saw too many musicals. Real-life was distorted for me because each story should have a happy ending. High school got better. I went with a group of friends my junior year and had a date my senior year. For senior prom I asked someone to go with me. He said he wanted to think about it. We went to dinner and he said, "If it had been anyone else, I would have said no . . ." and that's when I got so excited and interrupted him. "So, you'll go with me? Oh, that's great. Thank you. I was worried I wouldn't be able to find a date." He smiled and said yes. Years later he told me the truth. I interrupted him as he was going to say, "If it had been anyone else, I would have said no immediately. Because it was you, I wanted to think about it, but the truth is I don't want to go with you." He had already graduated high school and didn't really want to do prom over. Oops! He saw how excited I got and didn't want to crush me, so he went. We had fun, and I'm appreciative he went with me.

## What You Look For Is What You Will Find

Mary and I had been in a mentoring relationship for about nine months, focusing on her career development. One afternoon she came storming into my office unannounced. She was red in the face from a mixture of embarrassment, frustration, and anger. Pacing the floor with arms wildly flailing around she proclaimed, "My new boss is out to get me! *All* she does is pick apart *everything* I say and do. In our team meeting, she argued with *me* about the numbers in front of the team. I know these numbers better than anyone and she's going to question me about them? In front of others? If she didn't understand them, then she shouldn't use a team meeting as her own training session. I'm *sure* she wanted me to look bad. I bet she's trying to find a way to fire me." As we talked it was quite clear, Mary had collected her evidence to support her theory. She presented it well enough that anyone would agree: her boss was out to get her.

I knew I was only hearing Mary's side of the story. We went through coaching techniques to help her deal with the situation, find ways to overcome how she was feeling, and I even offered to role-play a conversation she should have with her new boss. She told me she wasn't going to have a conversation. Mary was closing the door to coaching and to developing herself, and my fear for her was she would lose certain relationships, or even her job, if she continued to have resentment against her boss because Mary was so negative. In fact, if my phone rang and I saw it was her, I didn't want to answer. She was starting to drain me. I knew I needed to tell her.

I love mysteries. I grew up reading the *Nancy Drew* and *The Dana Girls* mysteries. Even today, I still love to read a good mystery. I also love to watch mysteries. First the crime, then they look for a reason and suspects. The most important piece is the evidence they collect because this will prove the suspect to be guilty. I love when there's a twist. They come up with a theory, have a suspect, and collect evidence just to find out that it was a different person. This first suspect is supposed to be innocent until proven guilty, but many times we, like the show, find someone in our life to make guilty and then collect evidence to prove ourselves right. This is exactly what Mary was doing with her boss.

I had one more coaching trick to try. I told Mary she needed to become a detective with her boss. She looked at me a little bewildered as I explained she needed to find three "good," positive things her boss did. Mary collected enough of the "bad" stuff her boss was doing to prove her guilty, lock her up, and throw away the key. She was so fixated on the bad she was missing the good. I explained that it was easy for her to find the bad stuff because she was focused on looking for that. Mary disagreed. She was adamant she wouldn't be able to find three positive things; however, she at least agreed to try. To her surprise and mine, Mary found five things that week. I told her to find five new things for the next week. Reluctantly, she left and again, to both our surprise, she did. After four weeks of finding the positive evidence and coaching Mary, she started to see her boss differently. Remember that quote by Wayne Dyer, "When you change the way you look at things, the things you look at change." It was working.

Now Mary was ready to have a conversation with her boss. We role-played until she was comfortable. I waited anxiously to hear how it went. Mary came pouncing into my office with a smile beaming on her face and full of excitement like a child on Christmas morning who got the best gift in the world. "She doesn't hate me. She's not out to get me. She sees potential in me from the first week when we met. She was trying to push me— she wants to grow me!" Shame on that boss for not setting those expectations and having that conversation upfront.

I often tell people, "What you look for is what you will find." Mary was looking for that evidence to prove she was right. We're all like Mary. There are people in our lives we create an image or theory about and then we collect the data to prove ourselves right. If we want to think someone is out to get us, we will be right. If we think someone doesn't like us, we will be right. If we think someone isn't doing their job the right way, we're right. Whatever thought we can create about a person we will find the evidence to prove it right. But when we're looking for that evidence, we miss out on the other things—the positive actions or words from that person because we aren't looking for them.

We don't just do this with people we work with; we do this with our spouses, children, friends, neighbors, churches, politicians, grocery stores, the world. If we want to think people are "bad" because of the color of their skin, hair, or eyes, or their native country, disability, gender, generation, or personal beliefs, then you will find all the evidence you want to say "all these people" or "this person" is bad, mean, controlling, immature, self-centered, wrong, evil, a terrorist, and so on. Or maybe it's less complicated and you simply don't like someone or are jealous of someone, so you tell yourself that the person is a bully, liar, cheater, not genuine . . . and then you collect your evidence. We allow our own insecurities about ourselves to be what we use to judge others. If we don't feel like we measure up to whatever we want or need, instead of working on getting better, we look to tear others down. We could be missing out on positive people and situations because of this.

We also do it based on other people's theories or experiences. My husband and I had reservations at a new restaurant, and we were really looking forward to our date night there. We were told how awful the service was and the food wasn't that good. We let other people's evidence set our mindset for what we should be expecting. Right off the bat we started collecting data to support the bad service. When we caught ourselves, we looked for the good service. If we hadn't, we would have had a disappointing night. Instead, we had a totally different experience than our friends. The service was good and the food was delicious. Yes, it took a little longer to be seated, but that shouldn't be the first and only reason to apply negative thinking. It was a new restaurant, and we should have expected it to be busy, especially during the first few weeks of opening.

Our daughter was told to avoid a certain teacher in her high school; he was a "bad" teacher because he didn't teach well, didn't have much of a personality, and gave too much homework. Based on how her classes aligned, she was assigned this teacher. She would come home and share what he did wrong. We asked, what did he do well? Eventually, she stopped finding all the bad and found the positive things he did and how the homework set them up to do well on the tests. Over time, she saw him as a good teacher. She went into the school year thinking it was going to be a horrible experience but left thankful for being in his class.

## 💡 Personal Activity: What are you looking for?

What you look for is what you will find. Remember, we're all good at being detectives. We make up a theory about a person or a situation, then we collect the evidence needed to prove our theory right. We need to step back and look at situations differently or collect contradictory evidence.

What about you? Is there something or somebody in your personal and/or work life you have created a negative theory about and collect evidence to prove yourself right? Why? What would happen if you collected positive evidence? If you looked at that differently, what could you gain from making a mindset shift? What positive changes could come from looking at this person or situation in a different manner?

Journal about one or two things you might need to look at differently. Go back to your items where you identified when you have a negative view and a positive view. Is there anything or anyone on this list you need to look at differently at home, work, school, or church? Someone or something in the neighborhood, in your friendships, and the like?

Pick one to journal about them here: For additional journal pages, see how to get additional resources at the end of the book.

## Chapter 1: Formulate Your Thoughts

I choose to look at the following differently:

If I did what could be different for me or the situation or person?

What are some specific things I can START or STOP doing to make this a better situation or relationship?

## Don't Judge Others...

As I sat in the Dallas, Texas, airport waiting for my connecting flight home, I worked on writing training materials. Sometimes when I'm excited about what I'm working on I can get so focused that it's very easy for me to block out things around me. This evening my attention was broken when I heard someone ask, "Are you a Christian?" Immediately, I was drawn in and raised my eyes to see who asked the question and who was going to answer. When I realized some 20-year-old, young man was looking right at me. I asked, "Who me?" To which he responded, "Yes, you're wearing a cross on your necklace, aren't you? You obviously are trying to say something by that." I couldn't figure out by his tone where this conversation would go or why he was asking. By this time, our conversation had enlisted the interest of others around. I felt a divide in the air and worried an argument could breakout. I smiled as I replied, "Oh, yes. This is one of my favorite necklaces. My mom gave it to me for Christmas a couple years ago." Not having answered his question, he asked again, "So, are ... you ... a ... Christian?" After a careful pause, I responded "I don't know." He snidely replied, "What do you mean you don't know?" "I don't know because I don't know how you're defining Christian." A door opened for others to invite themselves into this conversation.

Luckily, there were no arguments, but maybe some strong feelings expressed at times though. As each person gave their own definition and examples of their evidence for or against religion in general, I just listened. Finally, they called for my group to board the plane. As I got up, I smiled and said, "It was interesting listening to each of you. This topic usually has some strong feelings on both sides. I'm a Christian by the following definition: I believe that we're created to be in a relationship with God, but sin messed that up. I believe that there's nothing we can do on our own to get to heaven. It doesn't matter how good of a person I am; I still mess up every day. I also don't believe there's a measuring stick to say certain sins are worse than others. Because of any sin I commit, I continue to separate myself from God. Therefore, I believe that Jesus is the son of God and that He came, lived a perfect life, suffered, died, and rose again so I can be forgiven. Because I've accepted that free gift, I am forgiven. I'm not perfect. I'm not in a place to judge others. I still sin and do things wrong. I try to live a life that's pleasing to God and to love others—even those I don't always like. I get it right some of the time, but not all of the time." I gathered my bags and went to board the plane. I looked back at the young man and he nodded to me. I smiled back and walked down the ramp to the plane. I was left wondering why he asked and if my answer helped him or not.

Every moment of every day we're in control of how we choose to act and react to situations and people around us. There are moments I do so well and there are moments when I don't, and I realize it right after not responding well. When we become emotionally invested in a person, situation, or belief it can be more difficult to see things from another perspective. For Mary, I could have sided with her since I had been working with her. I knew her, I trusted her, and I believed her. Because I was her mentor, I was able to ask the questions she wasn't able to ask herself: What other reason could there be as to why this boss is doing this? Could there be a logical reason? I wouldn't be able to answer that without Mary. She needed to change her mindset and ask her boss.

In the same vein, I can't tell myself or others that I'm a great singer if I'm not. Additionally, I can't be down on myself because I can't sing. That isn't helpful or healthy. My mindset needs to shift from *I stink at singing to I may not be able to sing, but I can speak, and I'm a great storyteller.* Mary could believe her boss was out to get her or she could see another perspective. Don't dwell in the perceived truth when it's negative or false when you're trying to make yourself feel better or look better. Program your thinking to something positive. Be willing to listen to the truth and take appropriate action. That might mean changing a behavior, asking for forgiveness, or forgiving someone else or even yourself. Take time to ask and seek another perspective and don't judge everyone by one standard . . . **but listen to the warning signs.**

Let me be clear: there might be valid reasons for some viewpoints to be what they are and stay what they are. Don't put yourself in a situation that will cause you harm. Be aware of the dangers if that's the evidence you're collecting.

When I was in college, I befriended a fellow college student, Frank, who was going through a tough time. Frank's mom was just getting out of an abusive relationship. His father wasn't in the picture and when he was it was argumentative because of his alcoholism. Frank felt like he needed to be there for his younger brother and two sisters to help mentor them and to help his mom with responsibilities with the house and bills. I admired that of him and wanted to help him. I've always been (too) trusting and wanting to help others. I had a car, and he didn't. I drove him home or to the store or found other ways to help. During this time, I had a boyfriend. We had been together for several years. This friendship with Frank was only a friendship but somewhere along the way,

Frank started to blur the lines of friendship and it became a codependent relationship for him. I didn't see the signs. Other people didn't either.

He had met my mom. My mom is the queen of knowing if someone is a good egg or not. She would warn me of certain people (boys especially) if she got a funny feeling around them. I would say that my mom was usually spot on. So, when he was able to get through my mom-force-field, where she didn't see or feel his evil, then you know there was no conflicting evidence to weigh.

First it was funny: I would be somewhere on campus and he would show up. What a coincidence, you're here too? Oh my, we must be on the same schedule. We have to stop meeting like this. I always thought it was by chance. I would go to my boyfriend's house and Frank would call saying that there was an issue on campus and I needed to get back. At that time, I didn't even know how he got the number or my boyfriend's address. Since he was a resident assistant like I was, usually there was an issue that I would need to get back to help handle. But then it wasn't funny any longer as it turned into him stalking me.

There were times when he would walk past my boyfriend's house over and over. I would drive home forty-five minutes to see my parents and there would be a note on my car from him. I even left the state to go to a camp on the East Coast and he called me there. Again, not sure how he knew exactly where I was. This is before cell phones with tracking or social media apps that allowed you to see where friends are. He even was so bold to ring the doorbell and want to talk to me at my boyfriend's house. My boyfriend's father could tell something wasn't right. I knew he shouldn't be doing what he was doing, but somehow, I just couldn't say anything. I know now this was beyond my own control and that I should have asked for help. I knew he was controlling me when he threatened to kill my boyfriend or hurt his family or my family. I had convinced myself that this was my fault. I was sure that I needed to fix this somehow by myself.

Finally, after camp, I was freaked out enough and finally told my parents and boyfriend's parents after he called me at that camp. When I got back to town, I told him we couldn't be friends because this was an unhealthy relationship. I reminded him I had a boyfriend and that I wasn't interested in him in that way. Going forward for the next couple months I had limited my interactions with him.

Since we both served as resident assistants on campus, we would have to see each other at meetings. I would make sure to sit away from him. I could feel him staring at me. For weeks he would still try to contact me. I ignored him. He showed up again at my boyfriend's house and his dad once again intervened. What no one knows is how I was feeling. I had lost weight, started to get bad grades, missed classes, withdrew from my family, friends, and boyfriend. I told everyone I was busy, had a lot of homework. I was distracted, tired, and depressed. I was always on edge wondering when he would show up again.

Unfortunately, not too long after that incident, he showed up in my dorm room with a gun. He confessed he couldn't stand not spending time with me: at that point as we left campus, I knew I was being kidnapped. For a few days, I was fully in his control. During this time, he raped me. (I was still a virgin.) The only thing I kept thinking was about my parents, my brothers and sister, and my boyfriend and how they were probably feeling. I prayed for safety. As he started talking about how we were now married in God's eyes, I used that to my advantage. I was able to convince him to let me go. Once I was free, I made a race to my parent's house where we called the police. I didn't tell anyone about the rape right away. I couldn't get myself to believe it let alone want anyone else to know. I was already not feeling very good about myself, and as I've learned as a victim, blamed myself. There were many what-ifs I kept thinking about. No amount of what-ifs could change what already happened.

Unfortunately, the court system wasn't pro-victim and the district attorney said it was my word against his. Because people saw us on campus as friends, the court would see it as me trying to cover up a mistake. The district attorney who was supposed to be my advocate said, "Are you sure you aren't trying to hide something? Are you afraid that your mommy and daddy are going to find out that you aren't their perfect little girl?" For the record, I was never perfect. For the record, this happened. For the record, I was tired and worn out. I was tired of fighting. Tired of trying to fit in and do the right thing. Tired. Tired of worrying about everyone else and what everyone else was thinking of me. There was no evidence that was on myside. I was the victim and would be for a long time. The court only gave him a six-month no contact order. The last words he ever said to me were, "One day I'll find you and I'll kill you." And I believed him. This is when my life changed. I left Chicago never to return—at least not to live there. For several months, not even my own brothers and sister knew where I moved.

I started to do the "right" thing by getting counseling. When I moved, I was starting over again, like in high school. How can this be? My life, other than the Frank situation, was good. Really good.

I had been living my faith, following God, being a good person. As the weeks and months went on, I felt, like many rape victims, dirty and unworthy. I started to wonder what I did to be punished. I told myself it was my fault. I told myself that no one could love me. And I told myself that I didn't deserve to be in the relationship with my boyfriend. So, I broke it off.

After that, my life took another turn. I started to make bad choices. My new church was very opinionated and judgmental. They made me feel unworthy to even go to church. So, I stopped going to church. It's one thing to be held accountable, another to be made to feel undeserving even for Jesus. So, I started to live the way I felt. I met a boy. He was a few years younger than me. In about a six-month timeframe, we dated, got engaged, married (eloped), and divorced. Not too many people know this story. I'm ashamed of how I lived my life and how I allowed myself to be blind to the signs around me. The total amount of time married was a couple weeks before filing for divorce. I never even had time to change my name and we never lived together. In that timeframe, I was told many things about him from some of his friends, including that he got another girl pregnant. I learned how he had an addiction to drugs. I was so wanting to be loved by someone that I allowed myself not to see the signs. I thought I could help him. I felt like he needed me, and therefore, that was love. I was more of a mother figure to him. But that shouldn't have been my role. It was while I was in the middle of this mess when I finally had to hit reset on myself, my core values, my life, and my faith. I didn't want to spiral into another bad situation and keep making mistakes.

I've learned that neither the rape nor bad decisions I've made define me. I made mistakes. I still do. Trust me on that. I've learned and grown from them. My family, close friends and God were a huge part of my being able to accept who I am and to grow from these things. My parents never stopped loving me, always accepted me, and kept encouraging me. My brothers wanted to protect me and still do; my sister just loved me for me (I'll always be grateful to you). My husband, who believes in me and treats me with the utmost love and respect, never held any of my mistakes against me. I owe a lot to my Heavenly Father who had never forsaken me and got me back to where I am and who showed me that healing and good things can come from bad situations. These things in my life made me stronger and better—because it grew my faith even deeper. I learned that just because I lived according to the rules and tried to be a good person, that wasn't going to stop bad things from happening. I wasn't exempt (I'm still not) from bad things.

Some people think that because I'm a Christian, maybe that should protect me from the bad in the world, or that if you do enough good works, you should have good things happen. That's not how it works. Life doesn't get easier because a person has faith in God. It simply means I've the promise of eternal life in a great place when I die.

A little over five years later, the Illinois district attorney contacted me and wanted to reopen my case. I was confused. What I learned was chilling. Another girl from that college had come forward, months after I left, claiming she was raped by Frank. Still no conviction as the courts did the same for her, giving him a no-contact order. This time the college asked him to leave. But five years later, they were investigating a third victim somehow connected to Frank, but her story ended in murder. They wanted to open my case as attempted murder. Their case was weak. No DNA, no weapon. I had already dealt with this. Panic and fear came flowing in as if it was happening all over again. The last words I ever heard him say to me was that one day he would find me and kill me ... and now I could possibly see him again? Did he kill her? Could he kill me? I had a family now with my husband and stepdaughter. My mind raced with what to do and it resulted in me becoming overwhelmed with the feelings I felt after being raped. The voice in my head awoke and started to tell me I was dirty, that my husband couldn't love me (even though he knew everything). It told me I wasn't worthy to be a wife or a mother. It even told me that God couldn't love me, that I had too much shame even for Him. I had already been through counseling to move past this voice and to shut it down. I needed to reset my thinking and fast.

My mindset should have been *he is a dangerous person*. While I've forgiven him, I wouldn't call him up and be his friend today. Furthermore, I can choose to be a victim of what happened to me or I can choose to be set free. For the first few years I was scared to go home and visit my family. I was still letting Frank control me. I was waiting for him to find me again. I lived my life in fear. If I allowed my mindset to go to *bad things are going to happen in life* and then wait for something bad to happen and tell everyone how I was right, then I wasn't going to be able to live life to the fullest or the way God intended for me to live. There are always opportunities for bad things to happen. There are also opportunities for good things to happen.

How I choose to live is up to me. What about for you? There are people or situations in which you have made stuff up and collected evidence to prove yourself right. Do you have a boss you think is incompetent? Do you work for a company that has a bad culture? Do you love your job? Do you like the people you work with? Is life fair or unfair? Is your spouse unreasonable? Are your children . . .? The list goes on and on of what we could say about others. We should think about it from another perspective, what can they say about you? How do you contribute to a situation or the relationship?

*If you are in an unsafe situation or have been a victim of rape or abuse, please talk to someone. There are confidential resources available at RAINN (Rape, Abuse & Incest National Network), 800-656-HOPE and online at rainn.org.*

## 💡 PERSONAL ACTIVITY: SELF-REFLECTING.

When you're given a new opportunity, do worries and doubts flood your mind? Can you talk yourself out of this new opportunity? Is it easier for you to turn down the chance or not even try for the new opportunity—a new job, a promotion, a new relationship, making amends in an old relationship, whatever it is—do you let the fear of rejection and failure dictate if you try? Where does this come from?

Write down the last time you had an opportunity present itself and you talked yourself out of it. What was it? What did you tell yourself that caused you to not go for it? What would have been the best case if you had gone for it? What would have been the worst case if you had gone for it and didn't get it?

Write down an opportunity that is coming up or one that you can create for yourself. What is it? What stands in your way of success? What is the best case scenario if you get this? What is the worst case if you try and don't get it? What is the worst case if you don't even try?

Do you make comparisons with what other people have? Their jobs, families, clothes, cars, confidence, looks, talents, etc.? Why do you do this? Instead, make a list of the things you have and celebrate those things. Be thankful for what you have and stop wanting what others have. If not, you will never be happy. There will always be something someone else has that you want. Ask yourself: What do I have to offer to my family, job, friends, others, etc.? Focus on your positive attributes, your talents, your strengths.

*What you look for is what you will find* also works when you're wanting something to be better than it is. I've worked with those in hurtful, abusive relationships. These aren't limited to dating or marriage; these include other family or friend relationships where one person is controlling in a negative manner and the other person knows it but doesn't want to admit it. Instead of seeing how unhealthy the relationship is, they hope the other person will change. However, they also believe they can change that person. They collect the positive evidence every time that person is "good" or helpful, which pales in comparison to every time that person is hurtful, degrading, belittling, or in other forms physically or mentally abusive. Every person is responsible for their own behaviors, actions, words, and thoughts. As much as many of us want the best for others, we can't change them. They need to want to change and they need to make the effort. I used to think the bad things that happened in my life were my fault because I didn't try hard enough to change the person or situation. Most of that resided in my self-talk.

## Understanding Mindset and Self-Talk

We're having constant conversations with ourselves all day long. Some of us even talk to ourselves out loud! My mom always said that was okay to do, as long as I didn't answer back. We all have self-talk while we're awake. There are many studies proving that when a person has more positive self-talk, people are more confident, motivated, productive, happier, and resilient. When we allow negative self-talk to enter our minds, it takes over for how we respond to things. Remember, positive self-talk doesn't stop bad things from happening, it helps us respond better to those situations.

## 💡 Personal Activity: So many things I have to do.

Make a list below of the things you have to do today or this week: *Examples include grocery shopping, filling the car with gas, paying bills, etc.*

Rate how you feel next to items on the list you created:

1 – Happy   2 – Annoyed   3 – Angry   4 – Grateful   5 – Nothing

There are many things we have to do every day or every week. Things that are necessary to live, work, grow, be healthy, be successful. Back in the late '80s I found the difference between saying I *have* to do something to I *get* to do something. I used to say I *have* to go to school. I *have* to go to work. I *have* to do the laundry. I *have* to work on that project. What I learned was when I told myself I *have* to . . . I didn't really *want* to. It felt like a chore or inconvenience to do these things. Or sometimes I had to do something because it was expected of me. I *have* to go to the study group. I *have* to unload the dishwasher. One day I realized that when I said I *get* to work on a project, I was feeling pretty good. So, I started to say I get to for all the things I *had* to do. I *get* to go to work. At least I have a job. And you know what: there are some great people I *get* to work with and see every day. I *get* to do laundry. I'm glad I have nice clothes (not yellow jumpers though) and I *get* to do my laundry from home. That's convenient. I *get to* takes me from *I have to* with a sigh of misery to a place of wanting, needing, and positiveness. I have to go to study group because that's what's expected. I should want to go to study group to better my learning. Through the years, other great authors and speakers have written about this same concept.

## Tell Yourself a Different Story

A technique I created originally to help me with my self-talk and mindset is to tell myself a different story rather than get upset in the moment. For example, when I'm driving and already doing five to seven miles per hour over the speed limit and someone gets right up almost on my bumper because they want to pass me, but there's no place for me to go, I used look at them in the rearview mirror and give them that look that said, "Back off, buddy," and if they didn't heed my warning, I might take my foot off the gas and go a little slower. Now, this is not the right way to handle this situation. It can make that person more upset and cause road-rage! Instead of calling that person a jerk and trying to teach them a lesson, I simply make up a reason why they're needing to speed: "I need to get over because this person must be on the way to the hospital to see a loved one before it's too late" or "This person must be late to work and they could lose their job. If they lose their job, how will they feed their fifteen children?" (The more children I give someone the more of a jerk they were on my tail.) When I change the story, I'm in control of how I'm feeling and reacting. Now I'm not upset. It also helps knowing as I move over and let them take the lead, they will weed out the police hiding miles ahead. Such sweet satisfaction when you pass that person and they're pulled over.

Where does self-talk come from? (Remember, I'm not a psychologist. I can answer this question from my point of view based on what I've learned along the way.) I believe self-talk comes from our past experiences that show up like a recording that we play repeatedly in our minds. We replay a memory and it reminds us how we felt then. If someone was verbally or physically abusive to you, you may remind yourself you aren't good enough or that you deserved that. Maybe it's from an old boss who never gave compliments and seemed ungrateful. The harder you worked, the less you were noticed. So you started to tell yourself that you're doing a bad job or you're not valuable to the team or that the boss doesn't like you. Maybe you asked seven people to go to a school dance with you and they all said no. You tell yourself you aren't liked or that you're strange or something is wrong with you.

Maybe you have an unrealistic idea presented by the world. Commercials, glamour magazines, social media, (fake) reality tv—all these things influence our thoughts and how we think of ourselves or what we think of others. Remember, your life's experiences make up how you view the world and view yourself. Your thoughts become the source of your mood, your emotions, and ultimately, your actions. No matter what the source is, when you play that video or tape recording over and over from the past, you continue to live it in the present and will never get away from it in the future.

The old or new voices that tear you down aren't helping you grow and become better. You must replace those voices with a new recording. It starts with what and how you think about yourself. What you think about you is what others will think about you. Once you think it, you act on it. One negative thought can turn into many negative thoughts. There's a snowball effect that makes it self-destructing: "I'm not good at test taking. This is so hard: look at all these things I have to memorize. I'm so dumb. I'm never going to pass this test. I'm going to be in school forever. I might as well give up on getting this degree." See how it festers and fosters more negative thinking. This is self-destructive.

Try it with positive self-talk: "I provided good input during the team meeting today. My idea saved the company money and time. It was a unique idea. I'm creative when it comes to problem solving. I'm valuable to this team." Being able to identify where your self-talk comes from is important. You might need to seek professional help through a counselor or doctor. Deal with your past so that you can leave it in the past. Remember, we can't go back and change the things that already happened. They happened. We can however be thoughtful in how we're living in the present and aware of how our decisions, words, and actions impact the future. Are you willing and able to create a new path if things are not going the way you wanted or needed?

More importantly is understanding how God sees you. He loves you so much. There's nothing you can say or do that will ever be enough to separate you from his love. There's no amount of shame we can carry that He is not willing to forgive or look past. No matter what happened to you or what you did, know you're fully loved by God. This has been my saving grace.

Here's how I changed my self-talk to be more positive:

- **Make a list of your strengths and positive attributes.** When I did this, I made sure to keep it realistic. (No, I didn't add singing to my list.) If I had a hard time naming them myself, then I asked others what they thought my top two strengths were. This also helped me get some validation.

- **Pay attention to when self-doubt creeps in.** When I started to have self-doubt and negative thoughts, I noted what I was doing or who I was around. I paused to ask myself why I was feeling this way or thinking like this.

- **Redirect your thinking.** When I stopped and asked myself questions to redirect my thinking, it allowed me to recover faster. Here's my favorite list of questions when I'm talking to myself. (I used these when coaching others also!)
    - Am I overreacting? Is this thing that big of a deal? How important is it to me in the long run?
    - Why do I feel this is true?

- What if it weren't true? What would I have to believe instead?
- What am I basing my thoughts/feeling on? Is this coming from me or someone else?
- What's a different story I can tell myself right now? If I believed that new story, what's the best-case scenario if that happened?
- Who or what is holding me back? What do I need to do move forward?

- **Change who you spend your time with.** I removed myself or people from my life who were complainers, consistently negative, or judgmental, or all three. Immediately, I could feel a difference when I replaced them with more positive, happier, more forgiving people. This applies to social media as well. I've unfriended myself from others who frequently posted negative things or only responded negatively to other people's posts. (Someone told me they were unfriending me because I posted to many positive things and made them look bad.)

- **Set goals—realistic and lofty ones, and then work toward them.** Make sure the long-term goal has several milestones so that you feel like you're making progress.

- **Make time each morning for devotions, prayer, reading in the Bible.** For me this has been the most important change I made. When I make time each morning for these, I already start the day better. On the days when I don't take this time, I'm off. While it's important for how

I think of myself, it's more important for me to discover what God thinks of me.

- **Find time to exercise.** Going for a walk, doing a quick video, videoconference with friends. There are many ways to fit exercise in if it's important to you. Exercise is not only healthy for the physical body but also good for the mind.

## There Once Was a Time for Me to Sing

When I was in eighth grade, I was in a play. This was a musical about traveling across America. We sang songs like "This Land Is My Land" and "She'll Be Coming Round the Mountain." I had the lead speaking role but not a solo singing role. In fact, my teacher had to rewrite the song parts when they were connected to my role. It's okay. I already knew that I couldn't sing. Then the most amazing thing happened. The night of the play, I had a microphone to use. It was supposed to switch off when we sang. But someone forgot to turn it off for one of the songs. I sang in it thinking I wasn't being projected. I sang without a mental filter for a moment. I sang as if I didn't stink because I thought no one could hear me. And you know what? I still was that bad, but no one said anything. No one made a face in the audience. The opposite happened: people clapped. I think a big part of that had to do with my own thought process. I wasn't aware people could hear me and so I wasn't reminding myself about how bad I was. I probably sounded a little better than normal, and at least I tried. When we remove negative barriers to how we think, we open the door to new possibilities.

## In Summary: Formulate Your Thoughts

When you feel negative thoughts sweeping in to distract you, remember the following:

**Seek to understand why you think and feel this way.** What is it about this person or situation that makes you feel this way? Is it based on your observations or did someone else share their experience, so you believe it to be true? What role do you play in how you feel? Ask yourself why you feel that way five times. This will help you drill down to the root cause. This only works if you're being honest.

**Example:**

Situation: Alice is unreasonable. She always wants to have things her way. I can't stand working with her. She's rude and treats everyone disrespectfully. She's only here to get ahead. Reporting to her is going to be the worst experience ever.

*Why do you feel this way?* She demands people respect her. She has a reputation of being controlling and selfish.

*Why do you feel this way?* She took credit for something several of us worked on. Others have complained about her behaviors, yet she got promoted.

*Why do you feel this way?* Because I have good work ethic and live our core values. She treats people disrespectfully.

*Why do you feel this way?* Other people who are just as qualified but better people could do that job.

*What are you actually feeling?* Some jealousy, frustration, unsure of the future.

*Why?* Others weren't given proper chance to apply for this role. She doesn't live the company's core values.

*What mindset shift do you need to make?* See her strengths and how she could have been the best candidate for the position.

*If you changed your mindset, what is the best possible outcome?* See where she's helping the organization. Know and see where I'm successful. Not holding a grudge and allowing it to make me negative. That others continue to see me in a positive manner and seek me for input. That I help create a positive experience for her. That my ability to be professional and positive helps me to gain additional responsibilities within my passion and strengths. At the least, I get to keep my job where I work with amazing people doing what I love.

**Look for contrary evidence.** You probably have collected evidence to support your thoughts/feelings for the negative situation. What positive evidence can you collect?

**Weigh the evidence.** Using both the positive and the negative evidence, do you still see this person or situation as you originally did? Remember, how you view this person is how you will talk to and treat them.

**Make a decision.** If I can't get to a point where I can be positive and open-minded with this person and be respectful to her, then I need to make a decision. I either need to accept that her core values aren't aligned with mine and deal with it (stop looking for the evidence to prove I'm right because then I'll continue to be negative and judgmental and likely turn others off by these behaviors) OR I can leave. If I can't change the circumstances I'm in, or my mindset, then I need to remove myself from them and find a new company that aligns with my core values and will allow me to flourish and grow—positively.

## Turn Your Learning into Action

How do you help shape the mindset of others in your workplace, home, school, church, or elsewhere when they have a negative view of a person or situation? Maybe it's something at work (job, customer, coworker, manager, process), at home (spouse, child, parent, in-laws, other relative, house, food, car, bills, etc.), school (teacher, classmate, process, topic, test, activities, etc.), or at church (the pastor/priest, the Bible, God, ministry work, etc.). Do you contribute to the negative thinking or do you help find contrary evidence? How do you help shape the mindset when you agree with the other person's point of view? What does this do for you or them if you're both negative?

Describe a negative situation or conversation you recently had with someone. What was it? Why was it negative? How could it have been more positive? How did you contribute to this conversation/situation? What could you have said or done differently to make it more positive?

Go back to the page where you identified a person or situation you need to change your thoughts on? Explore it further.

    Why do you feel this way?

    Why do you feel this way?

What are you actually feeling?

Why?

If you changed your mindset, what is the best possible outcome?

What is one new positive message you're going to start telling yourself about yourself?

What's one new action you're going to take to redirect your thinking?

# Chapter 2: Reinvent You

Can you see the face in the figure? This was drawn by a New York artist by the name of Paul Agule. What else can you see? Tilt your head and read the word. It says "liar." This chapter is about what people see and think about you.

**Your personal brand and reputation.** After having been a victim to things like a bully, hate crime, other crimes, abuse, divorce, being fired, losing friends, failing a class, losing a family member, being diagnosed with a terrible disease . . . whatever it is, once a person experiences these things, they're often a victim of circumstance. Not always, but for most of the people I know who have had these things happen, they're victims. I've been a victim to many of the things listed; however, I don't have to stay a victim. In the last chapter we talked about how to change our thoughts. In this chapter we will talk about how we change our words and actions.

I went to counseling with a rape victim counselor at a local university, and I met with a mentor from my church. I joined a small group as part of building trust with people again. I could have locked myself away and shut out everyone, which I did for a short time. I could have wallowed in my misery and let the experience define me, which I did for a while. Eventually, I chose to embrace what happened, and I used my experience to help others. I don't believe God wants bad things to happen to us. I do believe He can use these things for good. We need to be open to seeing how. The summer after my rape I went back to that Christian camp, as I had been for the past few summers. That year I had two teenage girls who had been through their own sexual assaults. One was date raped and the other sexually abused by her uncle. I would not have been able to relate to them or show full empathy if I hadn't been through what I went through. Being a victim doesn't define me. What happened to me is part of who I am, but it's not who I am. I learned so much about myself through that experience. I've my days—I'll hear something or smell something that takes me back to that time in my life.

When my daughter was in her senior year of high school, she received so many college and university brochures. When one came from my old campus, I stared at it. Thought about my experience. And threw it away. I know things like that can happen anywhere, but for my own healing, there was no way I was going to let her go there.

CHAPTER 2: REINVENT YOU

Can you relate to any of these pictures?

Hi! My name is Karen. I'm a crier. I cry when I'm happy; I cry when I'm sad. I cry when I'm frustrated; I cry when I'm mad. (No, I didn't mean to make that rhyme!) *And*, if you cry, I promise to cry with you at least 99.98 percent of the time. I can't help it. I've always been a crier. For a long time, I thought something was wrong with me because no one else I knew cried like I did. Maybe I need to clarify what I mean by cry. I didn't sob or cry hysterically. It could be watery eyes, some tears, or many tears. It was some form of empathy for someone else or true tears for whatever reason. It's a release for me in that moment.

One day at work, I had a peer ask to meet with me. I went to her office thinking she wanted training for her team since I led the training department. Instead, she asked me to sit down because she had some feedback for me. So, I sat. She led with, "I'm not sure how to start this, so I'll just tell you as it is. When people ask you how you are, we don't really care about the real answer." "Umm, what?" I asked, completely caught off guard. (I honestly thought we were going to talk about training needs.) She proceeded, "Yeah, we don't care if the dog ran away, or your baby was up all night. We don't care if you have a headache. All we want you to say is you're good, okay, or fine." I let her know I cared about other people's real answers. "Yes, we all know you care. But we don't," she said. I started to wonder who the "we" were she was representing. At that point, she asked me how I was doing. I thought it was a trick question, so I responded with, "I'm . . . fine." She said, "Great!" and continued her feedback. "The other thing is we don't like it when you cry. It makes us feel . . . well . . . uneasy. In fact, it makes us wonder if you will be able to take on more responsibility in the company or if you will stay at the level where you are. This could be a career stopper for you."

I sat and listened. This seemed to be a big deal, yet I wondered why this was the first time in five years I was hearing about it. Then it hit me, I bet people thought I would cry if they told me. Good news—I didn't! I didn't have much to say or ask at the time either. In fact, I was kind of numb. I thanked her and went on my way to process this feedback.

I'll come back to this story. First, let me ask you: Do you like to give gifts? I mean, will you spend the right amount of time to look for the right gift for the person for their special occasion? I love to give gifts, even if there's not a special occasion! Then, once I've the gift, I make sure to wrap it so it looks nice. Maybe add a bow, ribbon, or other add-on accessories or decorations. When I give it to the person, I want them to open it so I can see their reaction.

I want them to open it not because I want accolades but because I want the satisfaction of knowing I made someone else happy. When I make an awesome breakfast or other meal and bring it to my husband, I wait for him to taste it. I want him to take a bite and see his face. He knows this, so he messes with me by thanking me and putting it down. He makes me wait!

Back to the story. My friend gave me a gift that day. I had no idea others in the company, specifically the executive leadership team, thought or felt the way they did about me. She wrapped it and gave it to me, but it may not have been wrapped in the way I needed it to be. She had the right gift, just wrapped in the wrong words or manner—and because of that, I almost missed it. I went back to my desk, jotted down a few notes, and went back to work. That evening my husband and I talked about it. The next day I started to implement this feedback. When I was asked how I was, I replied with "good" or "fine" but never with the truth. Since no one else seemed to care, I stopped asking how other people were. I researched all kinds of ways to stop myself from crying. I tried pressure points—that only bruised my hands. I tried imagining the one person at the company I never wanted to see me cry: that only caused people to question my sanity as I would stare at an open seat in the room. I found one trick that worked for me then and still does today: *math*. When I start to feel my emotions stirring inside me, and not just ones that make me cry but anger, frustration, and sadness, I do math in my mind. It allows me to move to the logical side of my brain and away from the emotional side. Most time this works for me, as long as I make the math hard enough to try and figure out.

For weeks I was the new and improved Karen. Until . . . my team pulled me into a surprise meeting. Normally I love surprises. I felt like it was an intervention as I sat down in the specific seat they had designated for me. Everyone had their own place. All eyes were now on me as one of the women in the room took the lead and proceeded to say, "Karen, some of us have been with you for a few years on the team." Heads nodded in agreement while still looking at me. "Others in here waited patiently to get on this team because of who you are, or maybe we should say, because of who you were." Heads nodded again as she spoke. I studied their faces as I slowly moved my head looking at each of them. Another person continued, "We're having this meeting because we're concerned about you." Then another jumped in and with a high-pitch squeal blurted, "What's wrong with you? Is everything okay? You haven't been yourself. We're used to you asking us how we are, what we did over the weekend. You listened and you cared . . . but not these past couple weeks. You're different and we want to know why."

I started to do math. A lot of it! Some of their eyes got glossy, but they were able to hold back their tears. I continued to do math so that I wouldn't cry either. I didn't have an answer. At least not a good answer. How could I tell them that I allowed myself to compromise my own core values? This wasn't who I was, and it wasn't who I wanted to be. I'm not even sure how I answered because everything else that day was a blur.

I did some soul-searching that night. I was able to take two opposing views and the feedback each side provided me and thought about who I was and what I wanted to stand for. This lesson has never left me. More importantly, many of these people who then were my direct reports are my friends today. They showed a type of passion and concern for someone else, not because I was their manager. I needed to sort through all the comments and feelings and find the actual nuggets of feedback that I needed to hear and implement.

**Look in your blind spot.** Have you ever had something in your teeth like broccoli or pepper and someone tells you? Aren't you glad someone told you instead of discovering it later on your own and wondering how long that had been there and who saw it? Then you wonder, if someone saw it, why didn't they say anything? Maybe it wasn't something in your teeth. Maybe it was a bat in the cave. You know, a cliff-hanger peeking out of your nose. We're more inclined to tell someone when they have something in their teeth rather than tell them they have a booger hanging out of their nose. If we do try to tell them about the booger, we don't use our words. No, we send nonverbal signs, such as wiping our own noses hoping they will do the same. Some people just don't get the signs, they need to be told. (I'm not talking just about boogers either!)

Whether it's something in someone's teeth or the booger in their nose, if you're talking to someone with that thing there, are you really listening to them? Be honest – you aren't. You're distracted. You find yourself looking at that thing and thinking about it. If you're distracted, you may miss something important. That's what it's like for each of us when we have these things that everyone else can see but we don't know anything about it. For some of us, it could halt a career, break up a relationship, or cause us to lose our jobs. These are our blind spots. Wouldn't it be great if people told us about these things so that we could fix them or, at a minimum, be aware of how they were distractions?

I thought I was captivating an audience as I spoke to a group of women at a conference. Their eyes were on me the entire time. They looked like they were holding on to every word and letting the message soak in. I was feeling proud. Too proud. I was about to be humbled. After speaking, I ran to the restroom. To my HORROR I had drawn a line from one ear to the other from my lipstick that had been on my cup. As I drank from it, somehow the lipstick transferred from my lips to the cup back to my face. I looked like a clown. Here I thought they were listening to me, instead they were drawn (pun intended) to my new look. Ugh!

I'm grateful when people have a conversation with me about something I should be made aware of and how it could impact me, my career, a relationship, whatever. I've learned to listen through the tone to find the value the person is wanting me to know and receive. As I look back, I'm very grateful to both my friend and my team (of friends) who were willing and able to give me feedback.

Are you open to feedback? Do you want others to tell you when you have something in your teeth? If you do want them to tell you but you aren't open to the feedback, then you need to do something different. Perhaps you're unapproachable, and people don't want to talk with you. Maybe they avoid you. Maybe they don't know how you're going to react, so it's easier for them not to say anything rather than being subjected to your response. Maybe you're defensive as soon as someone tries to tell you something. You defend it or explain it away. You don't take any accountability, or you put the blame on someone else.

Even the most difficult conversations don't have to be. If you like and respect the other person, you're more likely to talk with them and share these things—because you care about them. When you don't like someone or don't respect them, you're less likely going to take the time to help them be successful by pointing these things out to them. The same is true if you don't like someone or if don't respect them when they give you feedback or want to discuss something about you. You're less likely going to take it as a gift. You might defend it, dismiss it, or avoid the conversation all together. You might self-talk about this person while they're talking to you. Nonetheless, the valuable piece of feedback is lost because of who is delivering it or how it's being delivered. If you trust the person, you're more apt to listen and take in the feedback, even when they're not saying it in the best manner.

We teach people how to approach us by how we respond to them. They see how you respond to others and assume you would respond the same way to them. It's important to be aware of our words, behaviors, and attitudes. It starts with understanding ourselves and our core values and how we live them. So, if you're not getting feedback (positive or constructive), you might want to ask yourself why. More so, you need to look in your blind spot by asking for feedback on how you're perceived. You can sort through the feedback to decide what's most important to apply.

**Start by understanding your emotions.** Through the years, I've read hundreds of leadership development and self-help books. In most of them, there are steps you should take to be a better leader, a stronger person, a more content individual, successful, happy, yada yada yada. Here I am, writing a "self-help" book . . . because I do believe in developing myself. I believe in you developing yourself. I've grown because I continue to seek feedback, read books, watch great speakers, try different things. A big part of developing yourself and growing is to understand yourself and all the things that make you tick, and tick you off.

I've heard this phrase so many times: "Feelings are indicators, not dictators." This is both similar and different than self-talk. When you feel a certain way, you should explore that to understand why. I like to tell my clients "don't ignore them [feelings], explore them," then let's figure out how to handle them. Your feelings may or may not be accurate. We're human beings and that makes us emotional. Many things can cause an emotional response. Some are things currently happening in the present and some things may be from the past. In my experience, when coaching people, many feelings that debilitate people come from worrying about things that they can't control or worrying about the unknown. So, when faced with feelings, sometimes we believe a feeling that may not even be real. This can cause us to respond or not respond appropriately. For instance, if you say good morning to someone and they don't respond or look at you, that doesn't mean the person is mad at you. Or if someone makes a suggestion for how to do your job, that doesn't mean they're questioning your ability or intellect. There are other reasons for these, but we jump to how we feel and convince ourselves that's the truth. Maybe the person didn't hear you say hello or had something else on their mind. Maybe the person making a suggestion just wants to feel included or noticed by you. What you feel may impact how you respond. Know your feelings, where they come from, and how to handle them.

**Start by understanding your priorities.** Priorities are another area we need to understand for ourselves. We're busy people. Each person reading this is in a different stage in their life. If you reread this again in a few years, you will likely be in a different stage in your life again. Some might be career focused while others are thinking about retirement. Some are more self-focused and others are more family focused. Some might be about getting immediate needs taken care of while others want to get things checked off their long-term bucket list. There's no right or wrong on where you are or where you want to focus. Where we get into trouble is when we're not balanced with our time and energy in the top priorities.

Before I had my daughter, I was career focused. I was focused on doing my job extraordinarily well and learning as much as I could, and I did have a strong desire to move up the corporate ladder. My time was spent working as much as I could to prove myself. I also surrounded myself with others who were driven, and I had some amazing mentors along the way. I still managed to do other things that were important to me, like going to Church, volunteering, and growing my relationship with my husband and stepdaughter. Up to this point, it was easy to manage both my career and family because we had Ashlee a couple nights a week, every other weekend, so I didn't have to feel guilty if I wanted to work late or bring work home on days she wasn't with us. When I finally got pregnant, my priorities shifted. I didn't want to work sixty plus hours a week, be on call twenty-four hours a day for my programs, take work home, or manage (directly or indirectly) the over one hundred people in my department.

I wanted to be a mom. I went from being a part-time stepmom to a full-time mom. I still wanted and needed to work, but I wanted to be an individual contributor who could do my job well and go home and be with my family. My priorities had shifted, and that meant I needed to make my first big career change. I went from being a regional training, quality, and recruiting director to a customer service trainer. It was harder for me mentally to go home on time and not work sixty hours since that had been my life for over seven years. Once I figured it out, I was a better employee, wife, mother, friend, and all-around person.

**Start by understanding your words and body language.** There are three big ways in which we communicate with other people: our words (what we say), our tone (how we say it), and our body language (our nonverbal cues). We're continuously communicating with other people even when we aren't saying a word. I coach people often on facial expressions, like rolling eyes, tightening of lips, and how they sit, fold their hands, cross their arms, etc. Every nonverbal either confirms what you're saying verbally or contradicts what you're saying, thus confusing the other person.

I remember once in a team meeting being called out for my body language. My manager just explained a new process we were going to follow. I didn't agree with it because there were so many issues with it. He was new to the team and making changes just to make changes. My body language confirmed that I wasn't in agreement with the change. He asked me if I had any concerns. I said no. After the meeting he explained to me why he asked me that. It was obvious to him I wasn't happy. After talking it though, he listened to my concerns and made some adjustments. I learned a valuable lesson that day—be aware of the message I'm sending, always. Since then, if I disagreed with something, I made sure to ask more questions to understand the why in the change and voice my concerns in a professional manner—always being aware of my body language and facial expressions. It's something I have to work hard at doing. My children will tell you I have a look that gives away how I'm going to possibly respond. Yikes!

Have you ever said something and as soon as you did, you wished you could take it back because that wasn't what you meant to say? It may have been the right words just spoken in the wrong tone. Try this in your head: When you read this sentence, what does it mean? *I didn't tell John you ate the last cookie.* When we read it, we take it for face value that you didn't tell John you ate the last cookie. When we speak it, the sentence could mean something different based on a word being emphasized or the tone used. *I* didn't tell John you ate the last cookie (I really didn't do it!). I *didn't* tell John you ate the last cookie (either they really didn't, or they're lying). I didn't *tell* John you ate the last cookie (I wrote him a note). I didn't tell *John* you ate the last cookie (I told Sally). I didn't tell John *you* ate the last cookie. (I told him someone did, but I never mentioned your name.) I didn't tell John you *ate* the last cookie (I told him you took it). I didn't tell John you ate the *last* cookie (I told him you took a cookie). I didn't tell John you ate the last *cookie* (I told him you took a cupcake).

One sentence can mean different things depending on how we say it. When you have a new puppy and it pees on your floor, do you say, "You bad puppy, you bad little puppy," with a high-pitch, fun-loving tone of voice? No! Otherwise, that puppy will think it's being praised and it's okay to pee on the floor. It's also true that you wouldn't say, "You good puppy!" in a stern, angry tone when it pees outside, or you risk the puppy thinking it did something wrong. Words matter and how you say those words matter. Words can build someone up or tear them down. Let your words and tone be a positive reflection of you.

**Start by understanding your level of forgiveness.** Forgiveness is an interesting word. Some synonyms include clemency, pity, mercy, compassion, understanding, leniency, humanity. Forgiveness isn't always for the other person; it's more for you. Maybe you have heard this saying before: holding a grudge is like drinking poison and hoping the other person dies. When we hold onto anger, resentment, grudges, hatred, the only person it's hurting is the person who is holding on to it. The other person may not even know you're upset and carrying around such feelings. Why talk about this? This not only impacts your thinking and how you formulate your thoughts, but it also oozes out of you and becomes part of your personal brand. You can't hide these feelings, and when possible, you will try to make them known to others. You try to actively engage others to feel and think like you're against another person. Sometimes it's out of sheer need to validate yourself and validate why you're holding onto the anger. There have been five major events in my life where I could hold a grudge, anger, and hatred toward others. By me letting it go, accepting what they did, and forgiving them, I'm the one who's free. I don't have to carry that with me, constantly remembering the pain, reliving the situation, and being negative from what happened. Some people say they can forgive but they will never forget. Don't get me wrong, I haven't forgotten what happened. I chose to deal with it by forgiving the other person and choosing not to replay it repeatedly in my mind. It does no one any good, including myself, when I do that.

## 💡 Personal Activity: Knowing yourself.

How well do you know yourself? How well do you manage yourself? Put an X in the boxes on how you would rate yourself MOST of the time.

**Emotions.** I can control my emotions. This includes all emotions: sadness, anger, excitement, frustration, etc.

    \_\_\_\_ This is a problem area.

    \_\_\_\_ I'm okay in this area.

    \_\_\_\_ This is a strength of mine.

**Priorities.** My priorities are defined and aligned. I spend the right amount of time with my priority areas such as: work, family, personal, health, volunteering, school, finances, etc.

    \_\_\_\_ This is a problem area.

    \_\_\_\_ I'm okay in this area.

    \_\_\_\_ This is a strength of mine.

**Body Language.** I'm aware of the messages I'm sending even when I'm not speaking. This includes my facial expressions, eyes, arms, walk, stance, sit, look, etc.

    \_\_\_\_ This is a problem area.

    \_\_\_\_ I'm okay in this area.

    \_\_\_\_ This is a strength of mine.

**Words.** I'm aware of my words and the tone I use when speaking. (I know when my words are encouraging or critical; I uses= words that adds value to others or situations vs. words that devalue them.

_____ This is a problem area.

_____ I'm okay in this area.

_____ This is a strength of mine.

**Forgiveness.** I can work past my hurt and disappointment and see the other person as a human. I am able to let things go and do not hold grudges.

_____ This is a problem area.

_____ I'm okay in this area.

_____ This is a strength of mine.

Go back and put a checkmark where you think others may rate you.

Was there a difference in how you rated yourself versus how you think others would rate you? If you really want to know what others think, ask people you trust to be honest to rate or give you feedback in these areas.

Choose an area you want to focus on growing this year.

What did you choose?

Why did you choose this area?

What do you need to do more of to be better in this area?

What do you need to do or not do to be better in this area?

If you did these things, what would success look like for you? How do you know? What would others see or hear?

## Identifying Your Core Values

One way to really get to know yourself is to understand your core values. Core values are a set of fundamental beliefs, ideals or practices that guide how you conduct your life, both personally and professionally. Each person has their own set of values or core beliefs they hold as their personal moral compass. Your core values steer you when making decisions, setting goals, and interacting with others. Others should know your core values based on what you say and what you do. Over the years my top ten core values have changed, but my top three have stayed consistent. This discovery process is enlightening to individuals and companies. Even if you have done this before, it's always interesting to see where your core values are now.

## 💡 Personal Activity: Your core values.

In this next exercise you're going to discover your core values. As you go through the steps, it's important to know **there are no right or wrong answers.** This is very personal, so make sure you're honest with your choices. As you work through this process, think about what represents your standards or qualities you believe to be most important to you.

### Instructions:

Before looking at a list of words to help you pinpoint words to use as your values, start by answering the following questions and make a list of the words that come to mind:

Think about decisions you've made in the past. Why did you make those decisions?

Think about people you've built lasting relationships with (personally and professionally) versus those you have not maintained. Why? What was it about certain people or relationships that were more important to you than others?

Think about goals you've set throughout your life— personally and professionally. Why were those important to you? Did you achieve them? Why or why not?

What's something you hold important to you? Beyond food and sleep, what do you need to feel fulfilled in life?

Describe a time when you were at your personal best. What were you doing? What strengths were you using?

Describe a time when you were frustrated, upset, or angry. Why? This is a good example of when you're not using your core values, or they're being questioned. What was being questioned that caused you to feel this way? Perhaps this is a core value of yours.

What are some characteristics that attract you to others? What is it about them that you admire? What is it about others when you're dissuaded by them? Again, this could mean a core value is in question.

If you're stuck, use this word list to choose words that are most important to you:

| Accepting    | Collaboration | Democratic    | Expertise  |
| ------------ | ------------- | ------------- | ---------- |
| Accomplished | Comforting    | Dependability | Explore    |
| Accountable  | Commitment    | Determination | Expressive |
| Accuracy     | Common sense  | Development   | Fairness   |
| Achievement  | Communication | Diligence     | Faith      |

| Adaptable | Community | Direct | Faithfulness |
| --- | --- | --- | --- |
| Adventurous | Compassion | Discipline | Family |
| Affectionate | Competence | Discovery | Famous |
| Agility | Competitive | Discretion | Fashion |
| Ambition | Composure | Diversity | Fearless |
| Appreciation | Confidence | Drive | Feelings |
| Approachable | Confidential | Duty | Fierce |
| Assertive | Conformity | Eagerness | Firm |
| Attentive | Connection | Economy | Fitness |
| Available | Consciousness | Education | Flexible |
| Awareness | Consistency | Effective | Focus |
| Balance | Contentment | Efficient | Foresight |
| Beauty | Contribution | Elegance | Formal |
| Belonging | Control | Empathy | Freedom |
| Boldness | Conviction | Empower | Friendly |
| Bravery | Cooperation | Encouragement | Friendship |
| Brilliant | Coordination | Endurance | Fun |
| Calm | Courage | Energy | Generous |
| Candor | Courtesy | Engagement | Giving |
| Capable | Craftsmanship | Entertainment | Goodwill |
| Careful | Creation | Enthusiasm | Grace |
| Caring | Creativity | Environment | Gratitude |
| Certainty | Credibility | Equality | Greatness |
| Challenge | Curiosity | Ethical | Growth |
| Change | Daring | Excellence | Happiness |
| Character | Decisive | Excitement | Hard work |
| Clever | Dedication | Experience | Harmony |
| Health | Learning | Persuasive | Reliable |
| Heart | Liberty | Philanthropy | Resilience |
| Helpful | Listening | Playfulness | Resourceful |
| Honesty | Lively | Pleasant | Respect |
| Honor | Local | Poise | Responsibility |
| Hope | Logic | Popular | Responsive |
| Hospitality | Longevity | Positive | Rest |

| | | | |
|---|---|---|---|
| Humility | Love | Potential | Restraint |
| Humor | Loyalty | Power | Results |
| Imagination | Maturity | Practical | Reverence |
| Impact | Maximizing | Precise | Rigor |
| Impartial | Mindful | Prepared | Risk |
| Improvement | Modesty | Present | Sacrifice |
| Independence | Motivation | Preservation | Safety |
| Individuality | Mystery | Privacy | Satisfaction |
| Influence | Neatness | Proactive | Security |
| Informal | Obedience | Productivity | Self-Aware |
| Innovation | Open-Minded | Professionalism | Self-Control |
| Inquisitive | Openness | Profitable | Selfless |
| Insightful | Optimism | Progress | Sensitivity |
| Inspiring | Order | Prosperity | Serenity |
| Integrity | Organization | Punctuality | Serious |
| Intelligence | Original | Purity | Service |
| Intensity | Partnership | Purpose | Sharing |
| Intuitive | Passion | Pursue | Significance |
| Invention | Patience | Quality | Silence |
| Investing | Patriotism | Rational | Simplicity |
| Inviting | Peace | Realistic | Sincerity |
| Joy | People | Reason | Solitude |
| Justice | Perceptive | Recognition | Speed |
| Kindness | Perfection | Recreation | Spirituality |
| Knowledge | Performance | Refined | Spontaneous |
| Lawful | Perseverance | Reflective | Stability |
| Leadership | Persistence | Relationships | Status |
| Stewardship | Thankful | Truth | Vital |
| Strength | Thorough | Understanding | Warmth |
| Structure | Thoughtful | Unique | Wealth |
| Success | Timeliness | Unity | Welcoming |
| Support | Tolerance | Useful | Winning |
| Surprise | Toughness | Value | Wisdom |
| Sustainability | Traditional | Variety | Zeal |

| Synergy | Tranquility | Victory |
|---|---|---|
| Talent | Transparent | Virtue |
| Teamwork | Trustworthy | Vision |

How many words are on your list of core values? If you have more than ten, this makes it harder for you to remember and live. Group your words into themes (words that are similar in meaning.)

Example:

| Integrity | God | Learning | Compassion | Accountability |
|---|---|---|---|---|
| Honesty | Faith | Growth | Empathy | Responsibility |
| | Spirituality | Development | Sympathy | Duty |

Use this space to group your words into themes:

Reduce your final list of words to ten. Force rank those ten words from most important to least important. When grouped in your themes, is there one word that stands out? If so, that's the group's core value for you.

Write your top ten core values below:

1. _____
2. _____
3. _____
4. _____
5. _____
6. _____
7. _____
8. _____
9. _____
10. _____

Defining Your Core Values: For this next section, focus on your first five values.

Core Value #1: _____

What is it?

How do I define the word? How would I explain it to someone else in my own words?

What are the behaviors associated with this value? How would others know what it looks or sounds like in action?

Core Value #2: _____

What is it?

How do I define the word? How would I explain it to someone else in my own words?

What are the behaviors associated with this value? How would others know what it looks or sounds like in action?

CHAPTER 2: REINVENT YOU

Core Value #3: _____

What is it?

How do I define the word? How would I explain it to someone else in my own words?

What are the behaviors associated with this value? How would others know what it looks or sounds like in action?

Core Value #4: _____

What is it?

How do I define the word? How would I explain it to someone else in my own words?

What are the behaviors associated with this value? How would others know what it looks or sounds like in action?

Core Value #5: _____

What is it?

How do I define the word? How would I explain it to someone else in my own words?

What are the behaviors associated with this value? How would others know what it looks or sounds like in action?

## Exploring Your Core Values

Our values are reflected in our choices—in our words and actions. Please answer the following questions:

1. For your top two to three core values, give an example where you have lived this core value recently.

2. If your family members, friends, or coworkers were to select your top values for you based on their experience of you, would they select the same values or different values? Why or why not? If different, what might they choose?

3. Are there any gaps in your daily behaviors as they compare to your values? What actions can you take to ensure that these values are represented by you in the future?

4. How do your values help or hinder you when it comes to your job/family/friends/school/other?

## Understanding Your Personal Brand

What is the first answer that comes to mind for the following?

A brand of chips: _____

    What's their tag line? _____

    Do you use this product or service? Why or why not?

    _____

An insurance company: _____

    What's their tag line? _____

    Do you use this product or service? Why or why not?

    _____

A fast-food restaurant: _____

    What's their tag line? _____

    Do you use this product or service? Why or why not?

    _____

A credit card company: _____

    What's their tag line? _____

    Do you use this product or service? Why or why not?

    _____

Advertising is a big part of branding a product or service. Branding includes the visuals, taglines, jingles, and then repetition of hearing or seeing these over and over. Even if you don't use the product or service, most of us can remember the branding. Just like branding may help us buy or try these products or services, so can reviews either confirm the purchase or stop us from making what could be a mistake.

Knowing your core values is important as it guides your words and actions. Does your character and reputation reflect these core values? What you consistently say and do become part of how people remember you and how they would describe you. If we were to survey your family, friends, coworkers, peers, or others who really know you, how would they describe you?

(This is like the review people would post about you to others.)

## 💡 Personal Activity: What do you want others to say about you?

If I were to survey your family, friends, and peers, what words (five or more) do you hope people would use to describe you? Put a star next to the words you're positive most others would say about you. Underline the words you need to work on because you aren't sure those would be consistently said by others.

**Answer the following questions:**

Are these words similar or different than your core values? If they're different, why were these not part of your top core values? Why did you choose them here instead?

For the ones you underlined, what do you need to START doing or STOP doing for others to start describing you with these words?

Are there other words others might have chosen for you that you would not want used to describe you? If so, what do you need to START doing or STOP doing to not have these words be used?

## Creating Your Vision

Creating a vision, setting goals, and then working a plan to accomplish those things is important for results you want in life, in a career, in a family, etc. Knowing your core values will keep you aligned for how you approach working toward the finish line. It doesn't matter where you are in life, you should always be creating and re-creating goals and visions for yourself.

When I was younger, I wanted to go to college and be a teacher. I went to college and stopped in my senior year. It would not be until fifteen years later that I achieved the goal of graduating with my bachelor's in business management. Am I a teacher? Yes, but not in the traditional classroom sense. I still used my skills and passion for teaching as a volunteer for Sunday school, youth group, vacation bible school, and local schools, among other places. I train adults across all generations for soft skills, leadership development, mindset shifts, and so many other areas. I get to coach people and help them see things differently and achieve their goals. But it starts with defining those things first.

I don't believe that if you imagine it, it can happen... I've imagined winning the lottery, it didn't happen. I can't win the lottery if I don't play. I can't make winning the lottery happen, no matter how many times I play or how many tickets I purchase. I can't will the lottery to make me win. While I can't control that, other things I can imagine and take action to make happen. I can imagine losing weight and I can exercise, eat healthy, and drink water. I imagined for a long time writing a book. Here it is. I visualized writing a book and took action. I surrounded myself with other positive people who reinforced the idea, I put a plan in place, and I set small goals. It took years, time, effort, and dedication to make it happen. You can imagine it and you have to put work into achieving that goal or dream.

## 💡 Personal Activity: Creating your vision board.

What are some of your goals or dreams? Make a list here:

**Create a vision board.** It can be whatever size you like. You will need poster board or a piece of paper to glue or attach pictures of your goals or motivational quotes. Collect pictures that show your goals and dreams—for example, if graduating college is a dream or vision, then look for pictures of college degrees, diplomas, pictures of the college or university, etc. Add these to your vision board. Is it a dream to buy a house? Get a car? Have a pet? Be healthy? Lose weight? Write a book? Have a certain job? Look at the list of things you created above this. Are these on your vision board? Find pictures or motivational quotes or statements in magazine and newspapers and print some off the Internet.

The next step is to attach these pictures and motivational phrases to your board in a collage. You can decorate it as much or as little as you like. Put the vision board in a place where you will see it often. Put the board in your bedroom, bathroom, office—anywhere you will be reminded. Visualizing these goals may help you achieve it. This is why so many people may put up a picture of a skinny version of themselves or a picture of an outfit they want to wear on the refrigerator as a reminder of what they're aiming toward becoming. When they get to the refrigerator, they have a decision to make. Am I making a choice that will help me achieve this goal or stop me from achieving this goal?

## Turning Your Vision into Reality

Now that you have your vision board, create actionable goals to achieve your vision. Start by prioritizing the things on your vision board and order them so that as you achieve one goal, it leads to the next. Take the first big goal and break into smaller goals. This will help you feel like you're making progress and keep you motivated.

When I finally graduated from college, I had all my children by then. I wanted to walk across the stage, not just receive a piece of paper. I wanted my children to see that when life throws you curveballs, you can still find a way to achieve those dreams. My mom also wanted to celebrate this achievement with us. She drove to Iowa, and we piled into a car and made our way to Arizona. This trip meant something extra for my husband and me. We have a goal to make it to all fifty states. This was going to check off ten states for us as we took one path there and a different path home. We also had the opportunity to visit several national parks and canyons. This became educational for the entire family. The goal was to drive to Arizona. That meant we needed a path to get there. We didn't just get in the car and start driving. We, and by that, I mean my husband, researched the drive and found places to stop and where to stay. We had a plan. State by state, mile by mile we crept closer to the destination.

Some people may have heard of SMART goals: specific, measurable, attainable, relevant, timebound. This can work for personal or career goals. For instance, when losing weight, you may set a goal and then like many people, get discouraged when the scale doesn't move as much as you wanted those first few weeks. Start with making the goal specific. You could say you want to lose 50 pounds, or you could be more specific and say you want to weigh 135 pounds. Can you measure this? Yes, because you will write down what your starting weight is and measure progress each week until you hit the goal. Is it attainable? Is the date and the amount realistic so you can achieve it? It's not attainable to lose 50 pounds in a week, not to mention unhealthy. Take your goal, make it SMART, break it into smaller goals or milestones to track your progress:

I will weigh 135 pounds by December 25. I will do the following:

- I will exercise 30 minutes 5 times a week.
- I will remove sugar from my diet.
- I will drink 8 glasses of water each day.
- I will increase vegetables and fruits.
- I will reduce processed foods.

Starting date: January 4. Starting weight: 175 pounds

I will weigh 165 pounds by March 25.

I will weigh 155 pounds by June 25.

I will weigh 145 pounds by September 25.

I will weigh 135 pounds by December 25.

Give yourself a chance to celebrate each milestone along the way to becoming healthier and make adjustments as needed. Each time you look at yourself in the mirror or weigh yourself it may feel discouraging. Until you lose that first pound. Then the first ten pounds. You can see your body looking different. Clothes fit better. You have the encouragement of others. Until . . . you achieve that goal weight. You look and feel better. You have the confidence to continue on this healthy journey. Hopefully, the new healthy lifestyle continues.

Do you have a goal for obtaining a specific college degree by a certain date? The school will help you break this into a plan. They lay out the courses you will take and in what order. You can follow your progress because you know what you have taken and what's left. It may feel overwhelming as you look at the long list and it may feel like four years is so long and far off. Then you complete that first class. Then the second one. Each time crossing them off. You feel excited. One year down. The second year over. You can visually see you're making progress. Until . . . you're done! You earned that degree. You graduated. You did it!

## 💡 Personal Activity: Turn your dream into reality.

Take a dream and let's make it a goal.

What do you want to achieve? Be specific.

When do you want to achieve it by?

Is this attainable? Can you make this happen realistically by this date? If not, what is a realistic date? What could be an obstacle for holding you back?

How is this relevant to your vision?

How will you measure the success of hitting this goal?

How are you going to achieve this? What steps do you need to put in place to make this a reality?

Who are you going to share this with so they can support you?

## 💡 Personal Activity: Reinvent your career.

This same concept can help you in your career development. Do you want to move up in your company, take on more responsibility, or go from an individual contributor to a people leader? That's great! It doesn't happen overnight. Set goals and create a career development plan.

What are you passionate about?

Where do you ultimately see yourself in your career? By when? Why?

What skills, knowledge, or experience do you need to attain to be ready for this position?

Keep in mind, your development plan, while made up of things to read, people to mentor with, jobs to shadow, and training to take, is only part of reinventing you and preparing for the next career move. Your personal brand in the company is also important to build. Ask yourself, How are you viewed by others? Early in my career, I was told, "It is all about who you know" in this business or company to get promoted. Maybe. There was also a stigma about women in most of the companies I worked. There were very few women leaders. I wanted to make sure I earned my promotions based on my performance and strong work ethic. There were many women who had the reputation of earning their promotion with who they got friendly with. Not all, but those who did made it harder for other women, like me, to forge through that stigma.

My very first company I started as a TSR—telephone sales representative. My job was to sell credit cards and death and dismemberment insurance over the phone. It was the highest paying job in that community at $5.25/hour. Higher than minimum wage at that time. And it was the wave of the future, so I was told. When I interviewed, I was taken immediately to sit with another TSR and listen for about thirty minutes. Then I met with the operations manager, Sandy. She asked me to read a paragraph from their script. I did. She asked if I could do what they're doing. I said I could. She asked when I could start. I said Monday. When I arrived on Monday, there was no one at the receptionist desk to greet me. In fact, there were piles of papers and folders all around it. It was a mess. I found Sandy and asked if that position was available. She said it was and had been for about nine months. I asked how I could get that job. She looked me up and down and said in a straight face, "Get 100 percent quality, have 100 percent attendance, and highest sales for three months in a row and you can have that job." "Challenge accepted," I said and held out my hand to shake. That was my goal. For three months I got highest sales (which I still, to this day, don't know how because selling over the phone wasn't easy), perfect attendance, and perfect quality. She held up her end of the deal and I was moved into that new role.

Within thirty days on my own I learned how to do that job. There was no one with the previous experience. No manual to follow. I learned how to audit I-9s, ensure all pieces of documentation were complete and accurate, worked through all the paperwork, filed it, and created some processes along the way. I even made a binder documenting how to do all of what I just learned. By the end of those thirty days, Sandy was surprised and pleased. Thirty days later she told me she was leaving the company. I was sad as I had built a relationship with her in a short amount of time. When the new operations manager, Jake was hired, Sandy took it upon herself to share with him about my strengths. When Jake took over, I became both the receptionist, the HR coordinator, and now his executive assistant all for $14,000 a year. Each time documenting what I did in case I wanted to do something else so that I could train the next person.

One day our director of operations, Don, came to the office. People were freaking out. I didn't know him or anything about him or his reputation. Apparently, he was known for not being a nice guy. When he walked into the office, I greeted him like I would anyone else, not knowing who he was. He looked at me and started to walk into the call center. I stopped him and asked him if there was someone he was here to see. Because I didn't know who he was, I treated him like he was any other person and would not allow him to just walk in the call center. He announced loudly who he was, and he didn't need me to chaperone him to see "his" call center. I called Jake to let him know Don was on his way to meet him. Fifteen minutes later Don came to my desk, sat on the corner of it and asked, "If I were a Styrofoam cup, where would I be?" Searching his face, all I could think was, Is this how he talks to people with riddles? What does he mean? My mind was racing until I got it! "Did you want a cup of coffee?" I asked. He said, "That is what I'm asking." In which I let him know the Styrofoam cups were in the cabinet above the coffee pot. Now he was the one who looked puzzled. See, I didn't know that he was really asking me was to go get him a cup of coffee. I'm very literal. He asked where the cups were, and I told him.

Two weeks after his visit, Don called me directly to let me know they were expanding in the corporate office. He was adding a training department and asked if I would be their first trainer. I said yes! I asked him why me. His response was interesting. He said it was because I was genuine and authentic in my words and actions. He was impressed that I didn't wait on him like a waitress and that I was organized while being personable. He had heard of my reputation for what I did on the phones and how I had organized the front desk and created training manuals. He even heard how I trained the receptionists at the three other locations so that we were all consistent in our process from call center to call center. He told me how he's around fake people who only want to know him because of his title and hope they can get ahead in their career. He was the one who told me that it's *not* about who you know in this company to get ahead, it's about who knows you and your reputation. Your reputation can make or break your career; therefore, always be aware of the reputation you create for yourself.

Sometimes I got it right, sometimes I didn't. I would tell you not to compromise your core values or your reputation. You will not make everyone happy—and that's okay. Don't let others influence you in ways that can lead to bad choices. Every decision we make, every word we speak is a choice. Choose wisely. Once you have said or done something, you can't take it back.

Here's how I manage my reputation and try to keep it positive:

- **List and define your core values.** My top three core values have stayed the same, but the others in my top ten have changed through the years, so I revisit this often. When I defined them, it made it easier for me to live them. When I shared them with others, it made it more visible to others why I did and said certain things and held me more responsible.

- **Be careful with whom you spend your time.** Sometimes your reputation is based on other people's reputation. My son was at home playing a board game with us when my phone rang. It was a neighbor who informed me that my son was playing ding-dong ditch and she would not stand for it. I asked her when that happened. She said five minutes ago. I told her that was impossible since Kyle was at home playing a game with us for the past forty-five minutes. Her only response was, "Well, he might as well be guilty since he hangs out with that group of troublemakers." What a great lesson for my son. He could pick up other people's habits, words, thinking, and reputation even if he wasn't with them. It was about how others viewed him. (For the record, this group of boys weren't troublemakers and they weren't even the ones involved.)

- **Set personal and professional goals.** This helped me stay on track for how I wanted to grow and succeed. I may not have hit them in the timeframes I wanted, but I kept striving toward that finish line, celebrating milestones, learning new things, and developing my skills. If I didn't hit a goal in the timeframe, I evaluated the goal and made changes so I could.

- **Ask for feedback.** We all have blind spots, and we don't know what we don't know. Just like the person who wasn't told about the food in their teeth or the booger on their nose, we walk around with things that are distractions to others and to our potential. We can't fix these until we look in the mirror and see it for ourselves. Find others you trust to be honest with you and ask them to be your living mirror. Tell them what you need from them and ask them for feedback.

- **Act as if a camera is always recording your words and actions.** I don't always pay attention to my words and actions until I've already said it or did it. I don't want the reputation of being a "Karen" as the meme states ("Karen" is generally characterized as an irritating, entitled woman, who likes to complain and ask for the "manager" when not getting what she wants or, perhaps, is not feeling heard). Are there times when I ask for a manager? Yes.

Do I have to ask in a way that draws negative attention to me or the situation? No. Can I ask for a manager when things are great? Yes. Do I need to work extra hard at my reputation because of this meme? No, not because of this meme, but because I strive for how I want others to describe me. I want to live my core values. I hope I'm already doing it right most of the time, but I know I mess it up sometimes. If I'm going to get upset over something, I need to remember: I'm responsible for my reaction. The other person isn't making me respond that way. Would I like this interaction to be replayed for others to see or hear? I know there are a few instances I wish I would have handled the interaction differently.

**Moving on.** If you go back and look at those pictures again and can relate to them, that's okay. It may look differently from person to person, but we all feel. Even the most logical person I know has shown their emotions; even the strongest person I know has shown their emotions.

After something difficult in my life happens, I allow myself a pity party. Let me tell you, I throw one heck of a pity party. But when it's time for that pity party to be over, then it's time to get serious, pick myself up, and get positive. This is when I start asking myself: How did this happen? What part did I play? No matter how big or small I contributed to this. What could I have done differently? What did I learn from this experience? What's next? How do I want to reinvent myself?

I worked for an amazing company. They had a great culture and great people, and they did a lot for the community. They still are great and still do great things. I had a peer who I felt went out of her way to intimidate me. Over the years we tried to make a business relationship work. On the day I was told I would be reporting to her, I cried. In my heart I knew this was the sign to start looking for a new job. When the announcement went out, I had vice presidents and other leaders contacting me, asking what I did to get punished. Some said I would only last six months. (I lasted longer.)

When she fired me, it was really for the best. I was so unhappy. I tried all the things I talked about in this book. Remember, there's no magic wand to make everything okay and I needed to not ignore the warning signs any longer. I searched to find positive evidence instead of collecting all the negative evidence on why I thought she was a terrible leader. Even if I found a few pieces here and there, ultimately, I couldn't get there. We would take one step forward and three steps back. I loved my team, the company, and what I did, but I was miserable. I was slowly changing, and I could feel it. I became depressed. I didn't want to go to work. I was starting to have bad headaches, I wasn't eating or sleeping well, and I was agitated and cranky. The irony of the situation is that someone put some comments on an engagement survey that I was blamed for writing. In fact, to prove I wrote them, she went person by person on the team and asked if they wrote them. When they said no, she had them sign an affidavit. I was the only one not asked and not allowed to sign an affidavit. While I maintain those weren't my comments, the outcome helped me close that chapter of my life and start a new one.

Instead of standing up for the right thing, I fed off of and into the negative parts of the culture. I can give you all kinds of reasons and excuses but that doesn't excuse me. I wanted so badly to blame her for all what happened to me, but I knew I played a part in it.

Blaming others is only excusing yourself. Placing blame is assigning your power to the person or circumstance. We say this person or situation needs to change for me to be happy. There will always be another person. Another situation. We blame our parents, spouses, children, bosses, teachers, friends, coworkers, politicians, strangers, the news, social media . . . In order to reinvent yourself, don't place blame. Take accountability. Make a conscientious effort to be better. We have the power to make better choices. We have the power to make an impact. It's not about title, or corner office. It's about knowing yourself, growing and developing your skills, mindset, strengths. It's about standing for something higher, doing your part to make yourself and others better, adding value to people and situations, and taking personal responsibility. It's about failing and getting back up and trying again. It's about inventing and reinventing yourself. Who do you want others to see you as? Figure that out and start living that out so others will see how you live your core values.

When I was fired, I had a week-long pity party. Three times in one week I had the same Bible verse show up three different ways. Jeremiah 29:11: "For I know the plans I've for you," declares the Lord, "plans to prosper you and not to harm you, plans to give you hope and a future." This verse has been my prayer and promise no matter what good thing or bad things has ever happened to me. Once I finally took some time to think about this verse and pray about it, that's when I started to reinvent me again, and with God's help, I'm better today than I was then.

## In Summary: Reinvent You

**Reinvent your reputation:** Start by discovering how others perceive you. There are many tools available for collecting feedback from others. If you think people will be honest with you, then ask them directly. Give them permission to tell you the truth. Make sure you're not defensive or explain it away. Listen. Take notes. Ask for examples. Ask what they think you could have done differently. It's also okay to ask when you have done something well, not only when you have done something that needs correcting. Most importantly, thank them. Look for trends as you gather feedback from others and make positive changes. In the past, I sent a follow-up summary of what I learned to those I asked for feedback, making me both transparent and vulnerable. In the end, it created stronger relationships built on respect and trust.

**Know your vision and build a plan to get there.** Plans may change. You may have obstacles that force you to go in a different direction. Don't give up. I've had many plans change in my life. My situation in college sent me on a totally different path for where I would live, who I would marry, and what I would do with my life. Just because I didn't fulfil my original plans doesn't mean I didn't create new plans and follow those through. Additionally, I am consistently making plans and new visions at different stages in my life. Be open to change. Be open to God's plans.

**Own your strengths and weaknesses.** No human being is perfect. Everyone makes mistakes and has weaknesses. Capitalize on your strengths, work on your weaknesses. Don't use your weaknesses as excuses. Surround yourself with those who have strengths that are not your own. Understand you will get farther with a team of people rowing together, all using their strengths for the betterment of the group, team, company.

**Do not become complacent.** The definition of complacent is being self-satisfied. Complacent people stop learning, stop developing themselves, and stop progressing. They become less motivated. They're less likely to take initiative. They just are. Life-long learning is key to growing and constantly reinventing yourself. What got you to where you are today will not likely get you to where you need to be in the future. Stay committed to personal growth and growing others.

## ☷ Turn Your Learning into Action

Who is someone who has had a positive impact on you and how did they impact you? If you have never told them and you're able to, let them know!




What is the most valuable piece of constructive feedback you have ever received? How did you respond to it initially? When did you discover its value? How have you applied this feedback?




If you were to do one thing specifically in your professional life that could have the greatest impact, what would it be and why?




If you were to do one thing specifically in your personal life that could have the greatest impact, what would it be and why?

# Chapter 3:
# Engage with Others

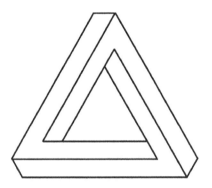

As you look at this drawing, is this even possible? Optical illusions can be fun for some people and annoying or tiring for others. This is true for how we are with other people. We may connect well with some and have a fun, fruitful, engaging relationship or interaction, while others drain, discourage, or demotivate us.

## When the Impossible Happens

In April 1976, two miracles happened in my family. My sister was finally here! She wasn't part of my parents' plan, but she was always part of God's plan. My mom had her tubes tied after my brother John was born. Don't get me wrong, I love both of my brothers. I just really wanted a sister. At church one Sunday, the pastor talked about prayer. I was too little to fully understand that not all prayers are answered in the way or timing we want or expect, but I heard enough of the sermon to know that God would listen. At home I closed my eyes and folded my hands and prayed out loud, "Dear God, I would like a baby sister. Amen." My mom immediately responded, "Oh honey, it doesn't work that way for how babies come to us." Six weeks later she would learn she was pregnant.

Fast forward through the pregnancy to the day Laura would join us. I was getting ready for school and my neighbor was over. I asked where my parents were and she told me the good news that a few hours before I woke up, my mom had a baby and it was a girl (of course, I expected a girl). I was so delighted! I couldn't wait to go to school and tell my friends. More importantly I couldn't wait to meet her.

After school I walked home with my two best friends, Lonnie and David. Lonnie's mom came out to meet us. He only lived a few houses down from me. I wanted to get home so I could go to the hospital. She stopped me and told me that my brother Jim had been in an accident and he was in the hospital. She explained that he was being taken care of but that no one was home and I had to stay with them.

I yelled at her and told her she was a liar and that my brother was fine. I ran to my house only to see where the accident occurred. He was riding his big wheel in the alley while my dad worked on our car in the garage. This was something we often did because of where we lived; it wasn't a dangerous alley. My mom was napping at the hospital; he came home to wait for us. A lady who was late decided to take a short-cut through our alley and going as fast as she was, she didn't see my brother. The car skid fifty feet with Jim underneath it. My dad had to lift the car off him.

There I stood looking at the blood-stained alley. I was now crying uncontrollably. Lonnie's mom carried me to her house. I sat there. I remembered God had answered my prayer for my sister so surely, He would again for Jim, right? I prayed, "Dear God, thank you for my sister even though I haven't met her. I need your help. My brother is hurt. Please don't let him die. I love my brother. Please help him. Amen."

My mom had a hard time in delivery but got through it. She was overjoyed with her last child (she forbid me to pray for anymore) and couldn't wait to bring her home. Our family was now complete. When the doctor told her about my brother, she got up and dressed herself. Jim was at a different hospital. They tried to keep her there. She said, "I'll be back. Take care of my daughter. She won't miss me yet—but my son needs me. I need to be there with him." And with that she found her way to the other hospital.

Jim had sustained major injuries to his foot that was down to the bone from the car dragging him. It had worn away his shoe and sock. He had major bruising, cuts, and other injuries throughout his body. The first forty-eight hours were most critical. The good news: he would survive but he would have a lot to overcome, including how to walk again. He was in the hospital for over three weeks. He even got to name our new sister. When he got home, there was a lot to adjust to: a new baby, crutches, and a two-year old (John) who was always full of energy. I had turned seven by the time Jim got home. My life changed that day, and I grew up a little faster because my mom needed help. I helped with laundry and she taught me to cook. I helped with housework and chores. I'm grateful I had this opportunity as it played a big part in who I am today. I'm also grateful God answered all my prayers.

Family is one of my core values. In my family, we're close. We argue and get on each other's nerves, but we also have each other's backs. We help each other, protect each other, support each other, and love each other—no matter what. This is one thing I'll always remember: as children, we were taught by my parents to respect others, to be nice, and to not cheat others but to find ways to serve people. Everyone. Not just family. When I think about this topic, how to engage with others, it doesn't take much for me to consider some people family.

## The Baby Porcupines

Jim had been recovering well. Laura was getting big. She learned to turn over and crawl. John was still rambunctious as a toddler and super smart. He knew how to climb things and take things apart and had the best hiding spots.

It was early in October when we went to visit my aunt and uncle in Wisconsin. Jim and I must have been driving my mom crazy because she sent us to play at the park while John and Laura napped. We lived on the Southside of Chicago, so to go to the park at the end of the street on our own was a pretty big deal. We got our coats on and off we went! Where we lived there weren't any sidewalks. As we walked to the park we stayed in the street, unless a car came, then we went in the brush until it was safe.

My aunt asked my mom if she was worried about us. My mom said with a chuckle, "No, all they need to do is see a stray dog and they will come screaming home." As soon as my mom uttered those words, they could hear me screaming, "HELP! It has him. It's eating him. Please, someone, HELP!" Neighbors came running out to see what was eating my brother. My mom and aunt came rushing down the street to see my brother dragging his hurt foot behind him. I could see it in their eyes they were both confused and scared. Scared because we were scared and crying. Scared because Jim was dragging his hurt foot. Confused because . . . there wasn't an animal near us. "What got him? What's eating your brother?" my mom kept asking. "The baby porcupines. They're all over his ankle. I couldn't get them off. They bit my finger." I replied in between sobs. Their faces changed as bewilderment came across . . . and maybe a little amusement. I didn't think it was funny. This was real and it was serious. They peeked at his ankle and on his socks were burs. We lived in the city . . . we didn't have burrs. I didn't know that was what they were. But from a seven-year-olds perspective, they sure looked like baby porcupines.

There are so many parallels to these stories and how we engage with people. Some people in our lives are family or close enough we consider them family. I understand not everyone has good relationships with their family. In my case, we're close. I was willing to pull off the tiny baby porcupines because they were hurting my brother. When that didn't work, I called out for help because I didn't want to see him in pain. When we get close to certain people, we have a tendency to want to protect them. When you care about other people, even strangers, your actions will speak louder than words. People we didn't even know were willing to help us. They came out with shovels, shotguns, brooms, anything to get what they thought was a wild animal off my brother. Why? Because people knew the dangers and if it were them, they hoped someone would come to their defense.

However, the same is true that there are some people in our lives who are like the porcupines. They bristle up and throw their spines at us, hurting us, and we don't know why. Porcupines do that as a way to protect themselves. We need to ask ourselves if we do this to others and don't even realize it, and when we are getting this from others, why?

Before my ordeal with Frank, I was a trusting, loving person. I am today too but I had to do a lot of work to get back to this place. Immediately afterwards I stopped trusting people. I stopped trusting myself. I stopped trusting God. It took me a while before I could learn to love others and myself enough to connect with people. Often though, I felt at any time I could be like that porcupine and push others away if I felt I couldn't or shouldn't trust that person. Building trust and rapport is something that came easy to me, and gratefully, it has again.

## 💡 Personal Activity: Your role in building relationships.

How do you build rapport with others?

When you meet people, do you think, "I wonder what they can do for me" or "I wonder what I can do for them" as you decide if this is a good relationship. (Personally or professionally) Why is that your first thought?

Are you willing to stand up for others when needed?

**Stand up for those who can't.** *While these next two stories are true, I'm not sure what I would have done had I not been through my own experience with Frank. I believe that situation allowed me to see things differently and to stand up for those who couldn't.*

Several years ago, I was out to dinner with a few girlfriends. We could hear a man raising his voice to a woman. He grabbed her by the arm and told her he would deal with her when they got home. Having worked with domestic violence victims, I was concerned she might be a candidate. She looked scared and didn't want to leave with him. As things seemed to escalate further, I grabbed a drink off our table and walked over to them. He had used her name so as I walked up on them, I said, "Sally? Oh, my goodness it has been way too long?" and I inserted myself between her and him. I gave her a hug and asked if she was okay? She whispered no. I asked if it was okay if we helped. She whispered yes, please help me. My girlfriend's husband was a police officer. I looked at her a nodded. She was able to get him to send a car to the restaurant. I was only a distraction for a few moments but enough of a distraction that he settled down and realized people were watching him. I don't know what would have happened to that woman later that night. I can tell you she had a different ending to that situation and for her life.

Once while shopping at Walmart, I came across this white male who looked to be in his thirties. He had jeans on with a T-shirt and a flannel shirt over the shirt unbuttoned. He wore a dirty baseball cap backwards. It wasn't about what he looked like; it was about what he was doing. He was crouched down behind an endcap, looking down the aisle. I glanced down the direction he was looking to see what he was so intently watching. The first thing I saw was a two-year-old child who wasn't being watched very closely. My mind raced wondering why he was watching this child . . . and when I looked over my shoulder, he was gone. I looked down the aisle, the child was gone too. I ran over and approached the person

I thought the child was with; she said her mom had her. Had I misjudged this person in the flannel? I went back to where I had been originally. To my surprise, there he was again—still crouched down and watching something or someone. This time I stood directly behind him and followed his gaze: two teenage girls, laughing and looking at makeup.

Please understand, this was right when we had two other teen girls who had been abducted and had been missing for weeks. As the teens moved to a different aisle, he did too. They went back to the other aisle, and so did he—and so did I. Convinced that this was his target, I walked up to the girls and asked if they were there with anyone. They said their mom and pointed to her. I told them to go to her now because there was a guy who was watching them. They ran to their mom, and as I turned around, there he was . . . six inches from me, yelling and pointing his finger, "Do you know what you just did?" The only answer I could give was, "Yes, I saved two girls from a creeper." He continued to berate me; now a crowd had gathered. I did what I do best . . . I cried. I was embarrassed and shaken from the incident. He was undercover security watching to see if they would steal makeup. How was I supposed to know that? He didn't have any identification and his actions were . . . creepy. He told me the next time I want to get involved I should go find an associate to help me. It didn't matter that I tried to explain my point of view as a mom and my concern for these girls. I'm sure these girls may have had a scare of their life, now knowing what if feels like to have someone watching them. If they were going to steal, they didn't have the chance and hopefully would think twice next time. For me, it was a good reminder that when you do the right thing, it's okay. Even if that means you're being yelled at and embarrassed by another person.

Some people have told me I should have minded my own business. Some people have said I was heroic. I'm not a hero. I wasn't thinking about me in those situations. I was a concerned individual who knew if something would have happened in any of those situations, and I could have done something and didn't, then I continue to be a victim in life always worried about me.

Look, we're all in the people business, no matter what you do. You can't escape people—they're all around us. Even if you are a student online, are a remote worker, have an office by yourself, or live alone, there are still times you will interact with others. Outside of work you see people at the grocery store, gas station, laundromat, restaurants . . . everywhere! Knowing how to interact with people is a life-long skill we all need to improve.

## Build Authentic Relationships

I believe everyone needs a friend—a *best* friend. Someone who accepts you for you, no questions asked. Someone who will belly laugh with you, cry with you, and just be there in silence with you. I've been blessed to have core people who are my friends and accept me, all of me, even when I mess up.

We also need people who are positive influences. Even my friends who say they don't like people will tell me they need *some* people in their lives. We weren't created to be alone. Even so, we can't escape people. Wouldn't it be better if we were nicer to each other? Showed more kindness? Extended more grace and understanding? Gave people the benefit of the doubt? Wouldn't it be nice if we treated people with respect and understood how we all bleed the same, not treating others according to skin color, age, gender, sexual orientation, weight, height, tattoos, hair color, and so on. We need to be authentic with others—even strangers. It starts by talking with people. Getting to know them. Sharing more about you. It also is how we respond to people. Doing this requires trust, from both parties. When trust has been broken in our lives repeatedly, it's hard to start over with someone new. There's that worry about when this person will hurt you, break trust, or just disappoint. Remember, what you look for you will find—so when you're expecting that, that's what you will get. More so, your own reputation plays a role in how you trust. What you say and how you say it also puts the other person either on the defense or allows them to be more open.

Think about these questions:

- **Do you start a sentence with a positive statement and then use the word "but" as you end it?** *I really like how you organized the project, but you should have had a column for changes.* "But" negates the first part of the sentence. Instead of "but," end the first sentence and start a new one. *I really like how you organized the project. One thing to add next time is a column for changes.* During a workshop, a lady raised her hand and told me that she learned about not using "but" a long time ago; she uses "however" instead. I told her "however" is a fancy "but" all dressed up.

- **Do you ask people for their insights and creative problem solving and then tell them it won't work?** The fastest way to disengage someone is to ask for help and tell them they're wrong. Make sure you're not creating an atmosphere that is negative and unwelcoming for people and their ideas. Instead, encourage idea generation and out of the box thinking. Use brainstorming techniques to foster collaborative problem solving. Always thank people for their input; don't call out why something won't work. This is true whether these people are family (spouses, children, siblings, etc.) or the people you work with (coworkers, peers, managers, etc.).

- **When you meet others, do you judge them?** First impressions are made within the first seven seconds of interacting with someone. Immediately, we begin to form opinions and judgments. It could be based on anything from how they look, how they sound, if they smiled . . . we start to collect the evidence and create a theory about someone instantaneously. I worked with a gentleman who wanted me to know he never judged anyone. Ever. I told him I believed he did. He told me to prove it. Challenge accepted. While we were meeting over lunch, a young girl walked by with a cut off shirt. I knew he had a daughter and so I asked him what he thought about her outfit. He told me what he thought, and it sounded like a judgment. I asked him if he was being judgmental. He thought for a moment and agreed he was. Why do we do that? It might be we pick out things in others we don't like about ourselves. Maybe we don't feel like we measure up to something or someone, so we find their faults. Maybe we have a standard we impose on others. No matter what, if what we look for is what we will find, how is that fair to that other person? Would you want them to do the same to you?

- **Do you reload the dishwasher or refold towels after someone else already did that?** Why do you do that? Because it wasn't your way? It wasn't efficient? I've taught my children that they can load the dishwasher any way they want because they know I'm going to redo it. I'm better now, but I wish I had been better a while ago. By me redoing what they already did sends a message that I didn't like what they did, therefore it was wrong; I can do it better, therefore there's no trust. When one party feels like they can't live up to another person's expectations, aren't trusted, or aren't valued, then it's not really a positive relationship. Their confidence and self-esteem are being attacked, even if it's in silence. At home or at work, it's okay to train others and explain why we like it done a certain way, or we can even change our own mindset, accepting that their way will work.

## 💡 Personal Activity: Your words matter.

Think about the last few times you used the word "but" in a sentence with someone. What were you meaning to convey and what do you think could have been interpreted instead? How could you have said the statement differently so not to negate the first part?

When asking for other people to collaborate on problem solving, which of the following will you explore further as a technique to use? Why?

- **"Yes, and . . .":** We say "no" often at home, at school, and at work. A positive way to build on an idea is to say "yes, and . . ." This is a technique taught in improv. It fosters a sense of cooperation rather than shutting down a person or their idea or the communication channel.
- **Positive Inquiry:** Positive inquiry is a tool and methodology that looks for the best in people. It opens communication, allows for more engagement, provides a learning environment, and fosters a conducive environment. There are exercises available to provide techniques for using this method.

- **Brainstorming:** This is a group exercise that fosters open communication to produce ideas or solve problems. There are several tools and ideas for how to brainstorm effectively. The premise is once an idea is shared, no one talks about why it won't work.

**I have a great idea.** I started a new job in 2006 in an entirely new industry for me. I was excited about the opportunity and to be working for this new manager, as she had a reputation for having great ideas. I'm a big-idea person and was hoping to have someone else to share in creative thinking. She called me to her office. "I've a great idea!" she was almost giddy as she said those words. "We're going to have our first ever leadership conference. We will invite all managers from across all states to join us for a three-day conference in Texas. And I want you to be in charge of it." I was a little shook. I had never overseen something so grand and wasn't even sure what to say or where to begin. Nonetheless, I was more excited and only a little overwhelmed. Here I was trying to learn a new industry, build trust with my team, get a handle on what we did to support the company, and now figure out a three-day leadership conference. My manager didn't leave me hanging. She came through on her big idea. The center of it would be John Maxwell. A small group of us would get certified in his 360-Degree Leader course and that would be the basis for our breakouts. More so, John himself would be the keynote speaker. Now I was even more excited!

A few weeks later, we were booked to Las Vegas. We spent three days learning the materials and everything we needed to have breakout sessions at this conference. This was my first visit ever to

Las Vegas. My manager thought it would be fun to take me to the Vegas strip. Our hotel wasn't on the strip and didn't even have one slot machine! Our last night, a few of us went to the heart of Las Vegas. We valet parked at Caesar's Palace. I was amazed at everything I saw. As we made our way to the valet to get our rental car, so were hundreds of other people who just left the Céline Dion concert. We waited and waited for them to bring our car. It was about forty minutes later when I asked what kind of car it was again ... and then it appeared. Finally! In we went! Just as she gets ready to pull away, we realize this wasn't our car. People are screaming for us to not leave. We had a good laugh.

I realized though that when you trust people who have proven to be trustworthy and have a solid reputation, you would follow them, even if it means getting in the wrong car. When you engage with other people, it's a relationship. In that relationship it calls for trust from all parties. In fact, John Maxwell's training was based on this concept.

**Bringing my learning wherever I go.** When we got back from Vegas, I worked on the breakouts and other things for the conference at home at night. It was the only way I could balance all the new things I was trying to learn and do and do them right. Each night I would tuck my kids in bed and set up shop in my bedroom. Scattered around me were my books and notes as I worked on my laptop for hours. Joe would come up and seemed almost a little jealous of how much time I was spending with John Maxwell. I told him that when the conference was over in May, I would not have any more distractions. The conference went well, and I held true to my word.

Shortly after, we took a family vacation to Disney World. Neither Joe nor I had experienced Disney World, so this was just as exciting for us as it was for our kids. We went with friends of ours who had been our neighbors but moved to North Carolina. As we walked through one of the parks, we were met with a rope indicating a parade would be starting soon. Yay! We had yet to see one of the parades. We had six children between us and put them upfront on the rope. Soon a couple more families joined us. We started talking about where we were all from, sports, kids, etc. . . . and then the parade started. It was superhot and super crowded. I could barely see because we had let all these other kids in front. I stood close to our children, and Joe was using me to steady himself as he videotaped the parade. And then . . . it started to rain.

Joe pivoted his body away from me to put away the video camera when all of the sudden some lady decided she wanted the space between his foot and my body. She checked me as if we were in hockey. Another push. Where did she expect me to go? I asked Joe, "Honey, did you want your spot back next to me?" hoping she would take the hint. Joe shook his head, and I knew he didn't want a scene. Another push. Wow. I decided to ignore her. Then . . . the . . . unthinkable . . . happened. When I didn't move for her, she took it upon herself to go around me. When she picked up my youngest child to move him away from the rope so she could stand there . . . I, I don't know what happened to me. I grabbed Kyle away from her and my hands were on her arms as I said in a very scary voice, "Don't touch my child," and then I realized, I train on sexual harassment, I shouldn't be touching her arms. So, I took them off but realized I wasn't at work, so I laid them back on her. All of a sudden, the two men from the other families we had been talking with emerged from their families and stood directly behind me. "Don't worry, if she gets past you, she won't get past us." one of them said. My husband is now watching all of this and asks me later, "How did you do that? How is it those two men were willing to be your bodyguards after only a five-minute conversation with them?" I blurt out, "John Maxwell says . . ." and now I realize John Maxwell is now on vacation with us. John Maxwell says that if you want to build a relationship with someone, it starts with a conversation. It's about how we connect with other people.

We do a lot of driving for family vacations and long weekends. Often when we stop, I'll engage with cashiers at the gas stations. Once I came back to the car and was very quiet. Joe asked me what was wrong. "That poor lady has to work two jobs. Her ex-husband is trying to get the kids away from her. She just needed a positive pep-talk." He just stared at me and said, "Seriously, why do people tell you so much about them? How did you have enough time to learn all of that in a matter of minutes?" I told him it was my gift. I'm a good listener because I listen with every ounce of me. People want to feel heard. They want to be understood. People want other people they can connect with. (John Maxwell's books and teachings stuck with me so much that in 2016 I became a John Maxwell certified Trainer, Speaker, and Coach.)

**Show you care.** Maybe you've heard this saying, *Nobody cares how much you know, until they know how much you care.* How do you connect with people? Do you care about others? Is it genuine? I was given the opportunity to have a young gal join my team. This person wasn't liked very much by the leadership team. I had questioned why they wanted me to have her join my team when I didn't even have an open spot at the time. I was told, "This person wants to be a manager in the company. She will never be a manager, and she is difficult to manage and too abrasive. You're really good at the feedback stuff. We want you to give her feedback and manage her for about ninety days. After that, you can fire her." I studied the director's face as I processed this statement. "I'm not going to do that. Either she gets a fair shot, or you can have my resignation. This is not how I operate, and it goes against all my core values." He told me to do whatever I wanted but that they warned me. As it turned out, this person never had anyone take the time to build a relationship with her; to get to know her as a person, or to understand her hopes and dreams. No one took time to find out why she wanted to be a manager. And no one took the time to give her praise or constructive feedback. As it turned out, while no one managed her, no one lead her either.

We started by building trust and rapport. Trust is critical before we could do anything else. This was a series of getting to know each other conversations. Eventually we created a development plan. We did a small version of a 360-degree feedback survey so she could understand her reputation. This survey measured how her peers, management, and customers saw her behaviors and competencies. I'm sure she was surprised when she saw the results. This allowed a starting point for her development. We met weekly to discuss how she was doing and what she was doing differently. Slowly she made little changes in how she approached people and situations. She changed the way she dressed. As her confidence grew, she became more approachable, and people sought her for her insights. She was promoted to a supervisor role within fifteen months. Nine months later she was promoted to a manager level.

I left that company, but we stayed in touch. She eventually left and continued to grow in her career, as well as personally. A few years later, she called me to tell me that she was going to be a president of a company. Here was the person who was told she wouldn't amount to anything in a company and now was leading a company. I didn't do anything except care about her. She did all the work. She had to be open to the coaching and make the changes. She just needed someone to believe in her at that company. I'm proud of her and glad we're still friends.

## Being Vulnerable and Transparent

How do you connect with people? Do you wish for friends? Do you pray for closer relationships? I mentioned it before, the concept of you get what you give. Engaging with others is a two-way street. If you want to be liked, you have to be likeable. If you want to be respected, you have to be respectful. If you want people to go along with you, they have to be able to get along with you. Connecting with others starts with you.

## 💡 Personal Activity: Connecting with People.

Journal about ways in which you connect with people. What are things you should start doing or stop doing to really connect with others? What would happen if you connected with others more deeply?

What does it look like when you're being genuine with others? What does it feel like when others are being genuine with you?

The more open you are to growing in a relationship, the more vulnerable you are to getting hurt. How do you feel when you read that sentence?

Pick one person you want to grow a more meaningful relationship with. This can be any type of relationship that may include a family member, a friend, a coworker, a neighbor, and so on. Now journal why you chose this person and what steps you can take to build a rapport with this person.

**Know your personality style.** There are so many personality style assessments and tools available. I like learning about myself and understanding my strengths, how I might be perceived, and how I might perceive others. I'm probably a little biased because my favorite is Real Colors® Temperament Instrument by NCTI (National Curriculum & Training Institute). I have been a certified facilitator with this tool since 2003 and a Lead Facilitator since 2015. After facilitating a Real Colors® foundation training one afternoon in Minneapolis, Minnesota, I noticed one of the participants, Bob, sitting at a table by himself while I picked up in the classroom. He was looking through the workbook and shaking his head. I asked if he had any questions. He looked at me and showed me a picture of his wife. "We've been married for twenty-three years." I couldn't help but notice some sadness as he looked at the picture. "Congratulations, that's great," I replied as I sat down. "No, you don't understand. Our divorce is going to be final one week from today." After an awkward gaze at each other, he continued, "Do you know I had no idea what she wanted and needed from me until today. I didn't *hear* her. I didn't understand her language because I was only listening through mine. It hit me during the brightening exercise. I wish I would have had this training years ago. It could have helped me be a better communicator. It could have saved my marriage. I would have been a better husband because I would have been able to say things differently."

We sat and talked for another few minutes when I got an idea. I asked him if they were amiable toward each other during this divorce. He said they were. With a bit of enthusiasm (those who know me will tell you that's easily done when I'm excited about something), I told him he should call her and take her to dinner and share what he learned. He looked at me puzzled as he processed my statement. Suddenly, the corners of his mouth formed into a smile that went all the way to his eyes. "Yes, I can do that." He wasted no time. Pulling out his phone he called her. His voice was shaky as he asked if they could meet over dinner. He told her he had something important to tell her that he learned today. He smiled as he hung up. "She's meeting me tonight!" We exchanged numbers because I wanted to know what happened. He left, and I finished cleaning the training room.

I thought about my marriage. My husband and I are definitely different from each other. While we have a great marriage, like all couples, we have our moments: disputes over little things of how something was said and how we interpreted those words or tone. No one is fully responsible on their own. He likes things clean and organized; I'm organized in my own way—ask me to find something and I can tell you which pile it's in. I like to hold hands and spend time together; he likes time alone. We had been married seven years when I was first certified as a Real Colors® instructor. When I went through the training, I immediately understood my spouse better, just like Bob. I couldn't wait for my husband to take the training. Real Colors® allowed us to better understand each other in ways that we didn't know we needed to. It has helped us to communicate in each other's language and to meet each other's needs.

A week later Bob called me to share his good news; they agreed to pause their divorce and, as he put it, date again. Through the years we talk occasionally. The last time I spoke with him, they were still married and celebrating thirty-one years. He shared how the training allowed him to see her for who she was, not who he expected her to be, and communicate the way she needed to be communicated with. Now, I'm not stating that Real Colors® will save all struggling relationships. I'm saying take training, read books, get counseling, stop looking at things from your point of view and learn to look at things from the other person's point of view. This isn't only for a marriage. It works with children, parents, sibling, coworkers, bosses, etc.

## ☀ Personal Activity: How do others see you?

People were created to be with other people. We need each other. If you want to engage with others more effectively, then you need to see you from their point of view. For the following groups of people, decide if they would say you're more often easy or difficult to get along with. Think about the evidence they have collected that would support this.

My boss or teacher/professor:

Would they say I'm easy or difficult to get along with most of the time?

Why would they say that about you? What evidence do they have?

What can I do differently to engage with them more positively?

My coworkers/classmates:

Would they say I'm easy or difficult to get along with most of the time?

Why would they say that about you? What evidence do they have?

What can I do differently to engage with them more positively?

My external or internal customers:

Would they say I'm easy or difficult to get along with most of the time?

Why would they say that about you? What evidence do they have?

What can I do differently to engage with them more positively?

My friends:

Would they say I'm easy or difficult to get along with most of the time?

Why would they say that about you? What evidence do they have?

What can I do differently to engage with them more positively?

My family (i.e., spouse, child(ren), parents, siblings, etc.)

Would they say I'm easy or difficult to get along with most of the time?

Why would they say that about you? What evidence do they have?

What can I do differently to engage with them more positively?

## Getting Others to Get Along with You

Adding value to others and making people feel important, respected, and appreciated also adds value to you. If you really do want to connect with others in a more positive way, to build trust and be seen as trustworthy, and to get others to go along with you, then try to **SHARE**:

1. **SAY.** Say what you mean, mean what you say, and don't say it mean. Be clear with your words and expectations; don't assume people can read your mind. If you want someone to do something, then be specific. Otherwise, the other person is going to fall short of your expectations. Additionally, if you say you're going to do something, follow through and do it. Your word is only good if you take action. Finally, make sure to wrap your message with the right tone so it can be received well.

2. **HEAR.** Hear others. Listen to what they're saying through their body language, tone of voice, facial expressions. Pay attention by putting away distractions and focusing on the other person. Look at them. Ask questions to get clarification. If you don't understand, say so. If you want to be heard, you must start by listening to others. One of the greatest gifts we can give to others is to be attentive, because it sends the message that they matter.

3. **APPRECIATE.** We need to do a better job of appreciating each other in this world. We can do this by acknowledging the efforts of other people. Pay attention

to even the littlest things others do that go unnoticed, not only the big actions they may do. Appreciate others by affirming their hearts. I feel we have more anxiety, depression, and loneliness around us and in us. People weren't meant to be alone. People want to feel loved and to show love. By affirming others, we're sending the message they're important, they're cared about, they're not alone. Additionally, be aware of what you say about other people because that speaks more about your character. Ephesians 4:29 "Speak only what is helpful for building others up according to their needs, that it may benefit those who listen."

4. **REAL.** Real is being genuine, authentic. Don't try to be something or someone you aren't to try to impress others or to hide who you really are. Be your best self by being real. When you're real, then building rapport with others will be easier. If you're real, then you will have more genuine, authentic relationships with others. If you want this from others, you have to be willing to give this to others.

5. **EMPATHY.** Not apathy. Apathy is the feeling of not caring. It sends the message you don't care. Dale Carnegie, author of *How to Win Friends and Influence People* wrote, "You can make more friends in two months by becoming interested in other people than you can in two years by trying to get other people interested in you." How do you make more friends and get others to be interested in you? By showing how much you care about them—first.

Empathy is putting yourself in their shoes and to try to feel what they might feel like. Empathy is understanding (likely because you have something you've experienced) and relating to the other person.

Here's how I build positive relationships with others:

- **Be genuine, generous, and gracious.** People want to connect with authentic people, those who are trustworthy, kind, and honest. Then when feedback is shared, they know it comes from the heart and with positive intent. I believe we're called to be generous. This isn't just about money; we can be generous with our time, effort, skills, talents, resources. Finally, be gracious. Treating others with respect, courtesy, and civility is so critical in building relationships and building up the person. Grace is an undeserving act of kindness. We have been afforded grace from God; we should afford it to others.

- **Find things in common.** We have more things in common with others than not. You'll find those things in common by talking with each other. Have you ever met someone you immediately felt like you didn't like or weren't going to like but then you discover things in common? Think back to how your initial thoughts may have changed because now you see them differently based on things in common. Find commonalities to bring us together and then celebrate our differences that make us unique and stronger together.

- **Choose people carefully.** It was a hard lesson for me to learn; I'm not going to be friends with everyone. There are some people who will tear you down instead of building you up. Some would prefer to use you and take advantage of your kindness and goodness. I believe in loving others and being helpful but not to put yourself in harm's way. Remember, you can't fix or change someone. They have to want to change. You can pray for them and support them, but they need to take accountability. Until that happens, choose where and how you spend your time with them.

- **Don't expect anything in return.** When you do something for someone, don't expect anything in return. Not a thank you, a favor, recognition from others, or money—expect nothing! This mindset allows me to help someone without any pressure of trying to impress them or have an underlining motive. If I don't expect anything, I won't be disappointed later. Help others because it's the right thing to do even if it's not the easiest thing to do.

- **Be an encourager, not a discourager.** We have enough negative messages coming our way. We have enough negative thoughts sending discouraging messages to our brains. People need to be encouraged. They need to know someone is rooting for them and believes in them. People want those genuine, authentic people. Be an inspiration to someone.

## Engage on the Level of the Person

When my children were little, I learned I needed to find a different way to grocery shop if I had them with me. Like normal toddlers, they would throw a fit if they didn't get something they wanted. If my child had a temper tantrum, I let them have it and didn't give in. Other people would get involved and give me unsolicited advice, like just buy it for them; shut that brat up, you're ruining my grocery shopping; take them outside; if you can't afford to buy it, I'll buy it for them ... wow. This is what's wrong in the world: we give in to the things we want to avoid. We give in to the complainer so that we don't have to listen to them complain. We give in to the bully because we want them to leave us alone. We give in to the loneliness so that we don't have to worry about rejection. We give in to the sin because we already believe we're unsavable.

When I was grocery shopping, I didn't give in, but I also I knew we needed to change things. I needed to find something that engaged them at their level. Something that motivated them. So, we set goals—compliment goals. I asked the kids how many compliments they wanted to collect on this trip. At home they earned points for positive behavior. Kyle is an overachiever and always wanted to collect one hundred points! Knowing that wasn't realistic, Morgan would suggest, "Let's collect five total and if we get more, we can get double points." Kyle agreed. Then we would shop. Morgan and Kyle sitting nicely in the cart, smiling, helping me find things... and then their first compliment, "Wow. You have such well-behaved children." And Kyle would yell, "That's one!" I usually had to explain what that meant. It worked for them because they knew how to behave to collect compliments, we got through shopping faster, and I was still smiling at the end. Finding what worked meant thinking differently and engaging with others, in this case my children.

## In Summary: Engage with Others

**Be genuine.** Live your core values. Don't try to be everything to everybody. You will please some of the people some of the time but never please all the people all of the time. Honestly, some of the things you might need to do to please certain people may not even align with your core values. Therefore, don't focus on making everyone happy, focus on being genuine and authentic and live your core values. This will make others want to engage with you.

**Add value.** People want to connect with people who are positive and will build into them.

**Be interested more than interesting.** Everyone has a story. There's a time and a place to share yours. When getting to know others, while it's important to be transparent and vulnerable with your story, make sure to show you're interested in the other person and their story. People want to be heard and understood. When sharing about you, don't try to one-up the other person, prove why you're awesome, or be boastful. Try being humble, sincere, and interested in others.

**Learn to SHARE. Say** what you mean, mean what you say, and don't say it mean. **Hear** others by listening to what they're saying and how they're saying it, including their body language. **Appreciate** things others do by acknowledging them. Even a simple thank you can go a long way. **Real** is being genuine and authentic. Be you. **Empathy** is showing care and compassion to others, to relate to how they're feeling. It's one way we can connect on a deeper level with others.

## 📋 Turn Your Learning into Action

What does trust mean to you? Do you trust someone when you meet them, or do they have to earn your trust? Why?

What does the other person have to do to break trust with you?

Is there any way to restore that trust? If so, what?

How does understanding trust impact how you engage with others?

Are there things you say or do that could break trust with others?

What do you need to START, STOP, or CONTINUE doing to engage with other more positively?

# Chapter 4: Energize Yourself

What do you see with this optical illusion?

It looks like it's slowly moving. I've to admit there are some days when this is how I feel—slow and messy. Each day I look for those things that energize me so that I can continue to serve others, do my work, be a better mom, wife, friend, and coach—really, to just get through each day. I find that when I'm doing tasks or spending time around people who drain me, I really need to kick my energy into high gear. If I don't, then I can take on those same negative characteristics. It's easy to pick up someone else's attitude when you spend enough time around them. Attitude is contagious. Once I'm depleted of my positive energy and good thoughts, then it's much harder for me to reset and reenergize. That's why I try to balance and surround myself with positive people: their energy is just as contagious.

Earlier I talked about how it's easy to fall into the victim mindset. When things don't go in the direction we want them, intend them, or need them to go, instead of accepting it or seeking to understand why, we would rather place the blame somewhere else or on someone else.

Maybe you have heard the saying "life is 10 percent of what happens to you and 90 percent of how you react to it." I believe the mindset you have sets the tone for how you respond to a situation. Your mindset impacts your emotional response to a situation or person. There are times when I can be in the best mood when something negative happens and it rolls off my back because I'm in a good mood. However, the same thing happens to me when I'm not in a good mood and I respond differently, by letting it get to me or by not being nice in my response.

The first part of this book focused on mindset shifts for a more positive outlook. I really believe that when a mindset is more optimistic or pessimistic, the stage is set for your energy level, response to a situation or person (thus your personal brand), how you engage with others, and your overall energy. I also am a big believer that your mindset is a big impact on your overall health, mental and physical.

**Taming my inner Karen.** One Sunday after church we told our daughters that if they were really good, we would go to a new mall that had opened near us and we would eat there. They were exceptionally good. I was about eight months pregnant and I looked and felt like it... When we got to the food court, Joe took Ashlee to get whatever she wanted. Morgan, who was three at the time, wanted something very specific: chicken nuggets, fries, a drink, and a toy. Hand in hand, we slowly walked by each food court menu... there it was! "Kid's special: chicken nuggets, fries, drink and a toy surprise!" It was meant to be. After waiting for about fifteen minutes, it was our turn: "She would like one of those kid's meals you have on your specials board." The young gal said, "Huh?" "The chicken nuggets, fries, drink, and a toy surprise," I read to her as I looked up. "Oh. Is that it?" I nodded and she gave me my total. After paying we moved to the next station to wait for our order.

Morgan is so excited as we make our way to Joe and Ashlee. I place her items in front of her: chicken nuggets, fries, and drink. She knows she must eat these before she can have her toy. But to my surprise, there's no toy in her bag. There was small piece of candy. I waddle back to the counter and waited in line, again. The same young gal asks what I would like. "Hi! I'm hoping you remember me and my daughter. We were here just a few minutes ago. We ordered the kid's special. She didn't get a toy in her kid's meal." The gal said in a tone that told me she hated her job, "We don't have toys here." I looked at her trying to figure out if they really didn't or if she didn't want to get one to give me. "Well, your sign says you do." And I pointed. She said, "Yeah, the sign is wrong. We don't have toys at this location." While it's a little silly toy, my daughter was looking forward to it. I didn't want to be a "Karen" and ask for a manager, so instead I offered some coaching: "Thank you. That's good to know. It might be a good idea to put up a sign or something so people aren't expecting a toy and kids aren't disappointed. We likely would have gone somewhere else had we known." She just started at me, so I smiled and left. I didn't use a mean or harsh tone. I wasn't nasty or rude. I was a pregnant woman with a disappointed child still trying to smile through it all—for everyone's sake.

As we ate, I noticed she created a sign, "Sorry, no kid's toys here," and placed it by the meal deal sign. It made me smile. I wanted to waddle back and thank her because I believe in positive reinforcement. I told my husband on our way out I wanted to stop there and tell her. Until . . . she looked at me across the dining area and said, "Are you happy now B!%$#?" Are you kidding me? Oh, this is it. My inner "Karen" is going to be asking for a manager. I got myself to a standing position and made my way to the counter. This time my waddle must have been loud because other customers could sense me coming up to the counter as they parted ways and made a walkway directly to the front, like the parting of the Red Sea. Even though I was fuming, I was able to ask calmly but sternly, "What was that? I was going to come up here and thank you for putting up the sign until you called me a B!%$#. That was uncalled for and very unprofessional." This young gal took two steps back. I'm not sure if she thought I was coming across that counter. Still no empathy. No remorse. No reaction. She had time to redeem herself. All she had to do was apologize. Here it comes . . . those words from a "Karen": "I would like to speak to a manager." "We don't have a manager." No manager? No wonder these teenagers have poor customer service. No one was there to train them, coach them, or support them. I knew my battle was a lost cause. I just smiled and said, "I hope you have a good rest of your day" and went back to my table. On the way home I called a local store in Cedar Rapids to ask about that franchise. They laughed as they told me they get tons of calls about how poor their customer service was. I thought to myself, all these complaints and nothing is being done. Their reputation will cause them to be closed in six months. I was wrong, they were closed in three months. Sad, actually.

I wasn't motivated to spark a conflict. In fact, I didn't want an argument or to be "that person" who raises their voice to get their way or asks for a manager. I was more motivated when a positive thing happened, and I wanted to reward that behavior. However, when that sudden glimmer of positivity was overridden by a negative statement, my motivation changed to addressing the issue. Still not wanting to yell and cause a scene, but at least coach for their sake, not mine.

In that story there are many lessons about motivation or lack of motivation.

1. **Expectations.** When we have expectations on how something should go, that can motivate or demotivate us depending on the outcome. For a three-year-old, there's not always the ability to reason with them on why something didn't go as planned. She had an expectation on a toy and didn't get it. How I respond is going to teach her how to respond. After my second trip to the counter, I told Morgan they didn't have any kid's toys but that she was lucky because she got to have her favorite meal. She smiled and said, "mmm, yum," and it didn't faze her. For

me, I had an expectation around customer service, and I didn't get it. Complaining about it wasn't going to change it. After I tried to talk to the girl, a manager, and another franchise, I let it go. At this point the only person it was bothering was me. I was in charge of how I was going to affect others—did I want my husband and daughters, and my baby who was probably feeling what I was feeling, to have a negative day or a positive day? They were going to pick up what I was putting out.

2. **Do what you love, love what you do.** It was obvious this girl didn't like her job. I bet her mindset about the job was "I *have to* do this" instead of "I *get to* do this." She wasn't concerned about her reputation or that of her employer. She wasn't motivated to serve others, be cheerful, smile, apologize, or take ownership . . . I don't even know if she was motivated to earn her pay. Why? There are so many reasons I could perceive to be true here: maybe the company didn't have core values for how their employees should act; maybe she thought her job wasn't important; maybe she didn't have goals and expectations for her position; maybe she had no guidance or coaching . . . maybe she just didn't care because she had to deal with so many unhappy, demanding, and rude customers that she didn't feel she was making a difference. Maybe she caught their negative attitudes. I believe that what you think about someone or something is how you will treat it.

Even in my first (real) job I was asked to clean the toilets (men and women). I don't remember that being part of my job description, but it was asked of me, so I did it. I cleaned those toilets with pride. It wasn't my favorite thing to do, but once I got praise for the good job I did from the owners and heard customers say those were the best cleaned bathrooms they ever saw, I was motivated to continue to do a good job every time. I had earned a reputation for "always" doing a good job at anything asked of me. This followed me wherever I worked. My work ethic became a motivator for me, even on days when I wasn't excited to do something.

3. **Someone else's lack of motivation should not be mine.** This girl didn't make me upset. I allowed myself to get upset. Yes, her actions and words weren't professional. Yes, things she said and did were uncalled for. People asked me why I didn't come "unleashed" on her and yell and scream so everyone could hear. For one thing, I didn't want my unborn baby to hear those things. I didn't want my children to see me that way. I didn't want to cause a scene. I wanted customer service. I didn't want my reputation to be that as a "Karen" meme, but to still live my core values. Did I do that? Not at 100 percent, but had I not been thinking about these things, I could have very easily unleashed my inner "Karen" on her and made everyone uncomfortable. But why? What did I have to gain? Even though her behavior wasn't motivation for me, my response wouldn't have been positive toward her and wouldn't have changed anything.

In the mid-nineties I read Stephen Covey's book, *The 7 Habits of Highly Effective People,* where he explains the circle of influence and the circle of concern. This is something I've been teaching, coaching, counseling, and reminding myself since my situation in college. I can't change that situation. It happened. I can, however, change how I respond to it. That response had a short-term and long-term outcome for my life. Same is true from this example. I can't change that the store didn't have kid's toys. Though, I could influence how they advertised it. Which I did. I couldn't change this girl's response. I could influence how I responded.

## 💡 Personal Activity: Know what motivates and demotivates you.

**Your turn: think about the following and journal your responses.**

What are the things that motivate you to do a good job at school or at work? Do you strive for positive feedback, to be acknowledged, to get good grades? Do you want to fit in and be accepted? Are you more motivated to accomplish something for you or to please someone else? Why?

What are things that demotivate you? Is it a person/manager/teacher you don't like? Is it a class or job duty? Is it the lack of acknowledgement or feedback? Why does this demotivate you? If you were to enhance this relationship or apply yourself to this job duty/task, what is one positive outcome you could expect?

**You are what you . . .** You may have heard the phrase *you are what you eat*. The phrase is intended to help us understand that our health is tied to what we eat. I believe it goes further than what we eat. I believe you are what you listen to, who you hang around with, what you read, and how you spend your time; therefore, if you want to have positive energy to give positive energy, you need to fuel yourself with positive thoughts, words, and people. Try a thirty-day challenge: change what you watch on television, what music you listen to, and who you hang around with. Maybe add in other things, like doing a daily devotion or spending time journaling. When you make these changes, avoid things that could be filling your mind with negative thoughts, fear, and other forms of discontent. Make sure to journal each day on this journey to see what your thoughts/words were on day one versus day thirty.

**Balance time and energy.** If I'm busy, I'm important, right? That's not (always) true. It's important we find some downtime; we need rest. This allows us to recharge, heal, and recover. This allows us to come to a different place outside our business, our jobs, our demands. Think about it: when we go to the movies or a play, they ask us to turn off our phones. Why? So we can enjoy the show, be fully present, and take a break from everything else—and to be respectful of others.

We enforced a rule at our house: no cell phones at the dinner table. Just because our world pings us does not mean we have to respond at that moment. When I was on maternity leave with Morgan, I had a pager. Our company had a rule that if the pager went off, you were to return the call within three minutes or you were reprimanded. I was on maternity leave and the pager kept going off. The purpose of maternity leave is to bond with your new baby. To rest your body after giving birth. I had been career and goal driven up to having a child. My focus changed. I wanted to be more present at home, not tied to a pager. About three months after going back to work, I was able to find a new company that allowed me to have a better work-family balance while going back to something I loved—training. If we're to be positive, make good choices to live our core values, and find ways to engage with others, then doing what you love is a great way to stay energized so you can do all these things.

## My Tips for Stress Management and Positive Energy

Staying motivated is sometimes hard to do when you're feeling stressed. Here are twenty of my favorite things, in no particular order, to do that allow me to manage my stress and be more energized when I may be getting near depletion:

1. **Practice an attitude of gratitude.** I try to always find things to be grateful for. I know this isn't a new concept and many people have written about this. There are studies that show correlation between those who practice gratitude and healthier, happier people. I like to make a list of at least three things I'm thankful for that day. I keep track on my phone. To challenge myself, I'll try to find three new things each day for a month, never repeating anything for thirty days. That helps program your thinking to look for the good, not all the bad. Remember, what you look for you will find. In my lowest of lows I reminded

myself of the good things in my life: God, family, friends, freedoms, opportunities, places I've been, people I've met, things I accomplished. It's easy to find all the things that are wrong in life. But when you seek out the good and count your blessings, you will see those are the things that really do count.

2. **Take time to breathe.** My watch reminds me to take time to breathe. I take several deep breaths in and slowly let the air out. For me, I close my eyes and feel the breath filling my lungs. It helps me relax and resets my mind. Taking time to breathe can also mean just slowing down. I go at a fast pace all day long. Sometimes I don't know if I'm coming or going. Breathing is something that we just do without thinking about it. It's also something we can control. Deep breathing is a technique taught with yoga and other forms of relaxation as a way to reset your nervous system. There are studies that link breathing to cognitive performance, reduces stress, and being healthier.

3. **Brush your teeth.** There's something about a fresh mouth. I have an extra toothbrush in my workbag. Not only does it help my oral hygiene, but it also makes me feel better and more confident. Another added energizer is the minty toothpaste! From a health perspective, this also helps you with cravings. If you're a stress eater, brushing your teeth may help with fewer snacks in your day.

4. **Forgive.** When you hold on to a hurt, grudge, resentment, or mistake, the only person you're hurting is yourself. If it has to do with another person, they may not know or care if you're upset with them. Carrying around your hurt, anger, frustration, resentment, or mistakes—or that of other people—is tiring, creates a negative mindset, interferes with how you engage with others, overpowers you, and traps you in time, reliving this feeling or memory. When you forgive, you're in control and gain back your strength. You heal from being a victim. Forgiving doesn't mean what happened was okay. You aren't condoning something you did or something someone did to you. Forgiving doesn't mean you have to let that person back in your life. Forgiveness means you have made peace with the situation, the pain, the memory. If you're holding on to something you did, you can ask the other person for forgiveness or confess to God and ask for His forgiveness.

5. **Set goals.** We've talked about goals in different areas of this book—for instance, when changing your mindset or creating your personal brand. Set a big goal, create smaller goals or milestones, and celebrate as you complete them. Goals motivate people and bring energy when they feel accomplished. If you find that you have some big items that are demotivating because they're so daunting or uninteresting, you should start your day working on those while you have more energy. If you wait until later in the day when you're less motivated, these things will continue to be daunting and uninteresting. It will take a lot longer to get them done.

6. **Share a smile.** This is something that is easy, free, and contagious. While it may seem like a small gesture, smiling and laughing can make a big impact on your overall health. Smiles and laughter decreases stress hormones and triggers the release of endorphins, which make you feel happier and more relaxed. Smiling is a way to connect with others, because it draws people in rather than drives people away. If you want to have a more positive mindset and reputation and engage with people and feel energized, smile more. Read a joke of the day or watch a quick video. Find a way to make others smile.

Joe and I were on a date night when he had an important call about something at work. Not a big deal to me because that gave me time to look at all the high-school students dressed up for a dance. There was this cute, shy couple in the corner. Neither of them were talking much, and both were looking down, then they would look up and smile and look down again. I smiled as I made up dialogue in my mind of what they could be thinking and saying to each other. I flashed back to my first date in high school . . . and how awkward I had felt. I smiled bigger now. Then I caught the eye of another lady looking at me. She smiled back. I nodded toward the cute couple; she glanced and smiled back at me again. Then another lady joined us, their husbands following along. Joe looks up from his phone, sees me engaged with smiles with these other people and asked, "What did you do?" I said, "Nothing, I just smiled." Smiles are contagious and you can't help but smile back at someone when they smile at you. Try to be upset and smiling. It doesn't work.

7. **Go for a quick walk.** Take a ten-minute walk. Make it a brisk pace, not too leisurely, but not something you're going to need to shower after or where you can't catch your breath! Walking is healthy for the body, soul, and mind. When I'm walking, I may listen to my praise music and sing along (in my head). I may think about a problem I need to solve, a conversation I need to have, or just not think about anything. Walking allows me to take a break and rest myself. It's especially helpful when I'm upset. I can walk it off and get back to a place where I can be more focused.

8. **Listen to something positive.** Listen to positive, upbeat, energizing songs or podcasts; stay away from negative messages. If you can't listen on your job, then add it to your walk or stretch time. When you have positive messages coming in, it helps train your brain to be more positive. For me, this includes not watching the news every day and definitely not before I go to sleep.

9. **Fill your water bottle.** Drink more water. Try to avoid too much caffeine and sugary drinks. For fun, add lemon or fruit to stay hydrated. (Try cucumber and mint leaves!) There are health benefits for drinking water. It's good for your body, skin, hair, and teeth. It flushes out toxins. It's good for weight management. It keeps you hydrated. There are studies that show drinking water makes us feel refreshed and improves our state of mind.

10. **Do something nice for someone.** I *love* surprising people, especially when they don't know it was me. If you aren't sure what to do, start by giving someone a compliment. Make sure you're genuine when you give it. Positive words help build someone and might be what someone needs in that moment. Mental and emotional distress is on the rise. We hear more about anxiety, depression, sadness, and feelings of worthlessness.

    In the last few years, I have lost several people to suicide. I worked with youth from middle school and high school for almost ten years at my church. The amount of suicidal thoughts and attempts were staggering. Even one is too many. Unfortunately, those I lost to suicide weren't the students but adult friends. This world does a good job of telling people how they don't measure up. Let's help people feel accepted and loved. Do something nice for them. Spread kindness. Saying someone matters is nice; making them feel like they matter is even better.

11. **Wash your hands with a scrub.** With the COVID-19 pandemic, we washed our hands a lot! This is different. Bring in scrub and take a few minutes to wash your hands with warm water. There are different scrubs you can purchase or make at home. Sugar scrubs add both exfoliation and a relaxing aroma. It's like a mini massage for your hands. When done, add your favorite lotion!

12. **Stretch/Stand.** Set a time for each hour and take ninety seconds to stretch or at least stand.. Reach for the sky and shake it out. This is a good opportunity to retune you. Take a moment to stand or stretch your muscles, fix your posture, reduce stress, and awaken your mind. It's like hitting a reset button, leaving you feeling refreshed. There are apps that you can download that remind you to do these and will tell you which stretch to do.

13. **Read something motivational.** Listening to something positive is one way to feed your mind. Having visual reminders in another way. Bring in a picture of a family member or pet or post a quote each day, or do both. Remind yourself why you do what you do and maybe who you do it for. Keep feeding your mind positive Bible verses, motivational quotes, or other stories to keep you feeling thankful and present.

14. **Work on a puzzle.** Sometimes you might need a break from the stress of the job. One way to give your mind and body a break is to do something different. Set up an area where there's a commune puzzle where anyone can take a minute or two to help solve it. If there isn't any space to do that, then work on a Sudoku or word find. Puzzles have been found to be a great meditation tool and stress reliver. They have a way of being relaxing. It forces your concentration to refocus the brain away from negative thoughts.

15. **Get a healthy snack.** I tend to eat when I'm stressed or bored. When I eat sugary, salty, or high calorie snacks, I'm left feeling nauseous and disgusting. The benefits of healthy snacks include controlling blood sugar, increasing nutrients (veggies and fruits), weight loss or healthy weight management, and reduced guilt later. Sugary snacks may give you some energy, but it's short-lived, leaving you sleepy and unable to concentrate and causing you to crash. Healthy snacks like fruits, vegetables, nuts, whole grains, or low-fat dairy products can keep you feeling satisfied, your metabolism regular, and provide your body with fiber and protein which acts like fuel that is slow burning all day long. Take time to be thoughtful in your healthy snacks and pack them to bring with you. Make it something you enjoy so you look forward to it. Bring extra to share and spread positivity.

16. **Send a note of thanks.** Another way to spread kindness, make someone's day, and to destress is to thank someone. This can be verbally telling someone thank you for something or to send a thank-you note to someone. The key is to be specific and share what you're thanking them for and why. Share the positive impact of what they did or said so that they can feel joy.

    Here's a challenge: Find someone new each week for fifty-two weeks, whether from a personal or work relationship.

17. **Exercise.** I've shared about stretching and walking, but exercising in general is good for the body and mind. Exercise gives so many health benefits, from providing stress relief, managing weight, and building muscles to protecting against heart disease and stroke. More so, exercise increases blood flow to the brain. This gives you energy and increases positive thinking. Make sure to check with your doctor before starting any new exercise program.

18. **Get enough sleep.** There are studies that show how important sleep is to our bodies and minds. We were created to rest. Sleep allows our bodies and minds to refresh. It's like when a battery is set on a charger overnight it has full power in the morning. Our bodies need to restore and rejuvenate in the same way. We will be better able to retain knowledge, comprehend information, articulate our thoughts and ideas, listen more intently, and focus on our tasks. We need sleep to build and store energy.

19. **Play with a puppy or kitten.** If this isn't your thing, that's okay, especially if you have allergies. There are reasons they use animals in hospitals and nursing homes. They make people smile. When an animal meets a person, they're accepting of that person. This might be what we all need. There are places you can volunteer to play with animals, or go visit a friend or family member who has one. They will cheer you up!

20. **Get sun and have fun.** I combined two in one! Find ways to have some fun. We all define fun differently. For some it could be walking, dancing, gardening, talking to a friend, singing, cleaning, riding a bike, painting, shopping, and the list goes on! Having fun is a great way to take a break from the grind of everyday responsibilities while allowing yourself to restore some energy. Adding in fun in the sun is a bonus! Sunlight boosts serotonin levels, which boost a person's mood and helps them feel more energized, positive, and calm. Aim for five to fifteen minutes of sun every day to balance out not getting too much harmful effects from the sun.

## Seven Types of People to Be Around

I've mentioned in this book about five times about how I surround myself with positive people. This is another way to have more positive energy. I remind my children that they become like the people they surround themselves with, so choose wisely. If you find you're becoming more critical of others, complaining about things or people, quick to be angry, or any other negative behavior, then you need to explore why. You can start by determining what about the situation is causing you to respond as you are. You can also think about who you spend the most time with and how they behave. It's easy to pick up other people's behaviors, words, or attitudes. Make sure you're surrounding yourself with people who will add value to you and be a positive influence. Here are seven types of people to surround yourself with:

1. **The Positive.** This person spends less time complaining and more time looking for the positive. They recognize when they're getting negative and can change direction. They look for the good in others and situations. They build you up, challenge you to think differently, and are that constant in your life. When you're down or negative, they're the person you want to call and get recharged.

2. **The Kind-Hearted.** In a world that is full of critical people, where people feel judged and cast out, this person will build into others and make them feel like they matter. They're genuine in the compliments they give. When they hug, they hug (even if it's a verbal hug). They want to help others when they can. They share their talents, time, and resources. They tell you the truth in a caring way to build you up, not to tear you down. They motivate you to be more kind.

3. **The Motivated.** This person is driven to do well; they want to be successful. They create goals and work to make them happen. They have a way of making others feel motivated to do something, be something, or try something. You can't help but feel inspired by them.

4. **The Innovative.** This person likes to find new and creative ways to approach problems, people, or situations. They inspire others to think differently, remove biases, and try new ways. They see problems as opportunities. When they fail, they see failing as having tried and getting to try again. They inspire others to go beyond the barriers holding them back, cheering them on the whole way.

5. **The Grateful.** This person appreciates the people and things in their life. They give thanks for all things—good and bad—and seek to learn and grow from all situations and people. They don't take for granted what they have been given or earned or people in their life. They remember to genuinely thank and acknowledge others for the little things as well as the big things.

6. **The Humble.** This person can acknowledge their strengths and will use them accordingly, but not for their own gain. They remember where they came from and how hard they have worked to get where they are but don't use that to judge others, only to mentor others. They use their strengths to help others and do good in the world without expecting anything in return.

7. **The Forgiver.** This person shows grace and understanding to others, even when the world tells them they shouldn't. This person likely acknowledges their own shortcomings and times when they need to ask for forgiveness. Forgiving may not be an instantaneous reaction, but in time when they have worked through to forgive, these people are the ones who are free to live and not hold on to negative feelings and carry a grudge.

Here's how I energize myself throughout the day:

- **Fill myself with positivity.** After all, positivity in equals positivity out. I typically listen to Christian praise music that makes me feel more energized and closer to God. This fills me with joy and keeps me focused. I've certain people in my life I can call when I need a pick-me-up. I start my day with a devotional, Bible study, and prayer. On days when I miss this, I'm off. Also, I find time to exercise, eat well, and breathe.

  My point is, I do certain things to fill me with positive thoughts which allows me to be more positive to others. When I don't do these things consistently, I'm not filling my gas tank with the fuel I need to be the best version of me.

- **Surround myself with the right people.** I don't always get to choose who I do business with or interact with throughout the day. I find that I have many people who drain me because they're negative or a victim-thinker, or constantly finding fault and placing blame on everyone else. When coaching these individuals, I can become depleted fast if I allow myself to go there with them. Instead, I balance those meetings with one of my seven types of people when I need a pick me up. I've certain people I call that represent one or more of those seven I mentioned earlier.

- **Remind myself everyone has baggage or a story.** When someone is negative, in a bad mood, or downright rude, I remind myself that everyone has something they're carrying around. While it may explain their behavior, it doesn't excuse it. However, what if I can be that person to make them feel accepted, heard, or loved? What if a simple gesture of kindness made an impact to them—even if it's only for that moment? It's easy to be nice to people who are nice, and it's easy to be standoffish to those who come across short, rude, abrasive, or negative. When I purposely go out of my way to be extra nice to someone who isn't being nice to me or others, I do it because I can and because maybe it will make a difference.

- **Forgive myself.** We've talked about learning to forgive others and not to hold grudges against people because it only hurts you. What about you? Do you hang on to your mistakes and keep reminding yourself of them?

## Don't Hold Mistakes against Others or Yourself

When my mom and dad were first married, my mom was tasked with making the pumpkin pies for their first family Thanksgiving at my grandparent's house. She had made pumpkin pies before and she went into the task confidently. She had a vision of how many pies, and she planned what she needed. She even envisioned making my dad proud as people ate her pies and smiled. She had collected many compliments in the past about her recipe.

Unfortunately, to her dismay, her pumpkin pies turned out white. She stared at them in disbelief. Where did she go wrong? After rethinking her steps, she found she forgot the molasses! Somewhere in time she shared this story with the four of us kids as we were growing up. For whatever reason, we always thought it was funny to remind her about her mistake when it was time to make pumpkin pies. "Don't forget the molasses," we would tell her, spoken as if we had been there when it happened. Lucky for us, my mom has a great sense of humor.

So, what are the two lessons we can get from this story? First, it's okay to make mistakes. This is how we learn and grow. Mom learned from her mistake and was more careful when using new recipes. *And* she makes awesome pumpkin pies. It's when you keep making the same mistakes over and over that it becomes a problem. If you do not improve or stop whatever that mistake is, then you risk the chance of hurting your brand, your career, or your own self-esteem. If you find yourself making the same mistakes or if you keep getting the same type of improvement feedback, then ask for help.

Second, what mistakes have you made that you continue to remind yourself about and beat yourself up over? Or what mistakes have others made that you constantly remind them about? We had no right to tease our mom about her mistake. It happened once and she improved. When we remind ourselves or others about a mistake, then we don't allow the healing and learning process to happen. Make mistakes, learn, and change so that you don't repeat. Move on; be the best *you* you can be and help others be the best they can be. Support one another and celebrate when someone grows from a mistake. What mistake are you holding yourself to?

## In Summary: Energize Yourself

**Identify your stressors.** Learn what stresses you out and implement some of the tips to dealing with stress. When you can feel more in control of your thoughts and reactions to stress, you will feel more energized and able to accomplish your tasks or goals.

**Pick positive people.** Look for people who can be any of the seven types of people to surround yourself with and make them a part of your life. Additionally, find which of these seven types you can be for others and start living that way so you can be a positive person to someone else.

**Input positivity to output positivity.** Remember to eat healthy, get enough sleep, and decide if you need to change the things you're listening to and who you spend your time with to decrease negativity in your life. When you're more positive, you will have more energy.

## Turn Your Learning into Action

What are things you do that drain/demotivate others? What impact does that have on them and you? How do you know? Journal about a specific person or situation where you demotivated someone and how you could have handled it differently. What would have been the outcome for them and for you if you had approached them in a more positive way? What are things you do that energize/motivate others? What impact does that have on them and you? How do you know? Journal about a specific person that you were able to energize.

What are three things you can do more of to keep yourself positive and more energized?

What are three things you need to do less of to keep yourself positive and more energized?

# Conclusion

During the COVID-19 pandemic, we've seen how people's mindsets and hearts are shaped. People are on one side or the other: "Is it real or is it a conspiracy?" or people view how it should have been handled by local, state, and federal government. During the first round of COVID-19 when I read comments on our governor's live updates, it was both astonishing and sickening to read such negative comments from every point of view, whether it was political, personal, or spiritual; whether it was about keeping people safe or keeping businesses in business. People responded to other people without considering the other person's perspective. They responded on why the other person was wrong and why they were right. No empathy for either side. The more the comments went on, the angrier, meaner, and more disrespectful people became. If someone posted a positive statement, others laughed at it, or made a derogatory comment. The truth is, there was no right answer that fit everyone equally. Instead of finding a solution and working together, people took sides and shamed each other. Shaming people for wearing masks, shaming people for not wearing masks. Shaming people if they were vaccinated, shaming people if they weren't. Shaming people for being positive, shaming people for being negative. Even shaming people if they got sick . . .

Then there were many people who made sure to thank the frontline workers; people who made sure seniors in high school had their proms and graduations, as well as college graduations; people who made sure to spread the word to be *kind* and that *hope* wasn't cancelled; and people who made sure people weren't feeling alone. Some people took the "extra" time we were given to reconnect with family, to learn something new, to get into better shape and health, to give back to others, to go to church for the first time or get back to church, to do something positive. Where were you? Were you on the one side expressing your feelings and using your constitutional right for freedom of speech to be positive or negative? What image did you leave behind to others in your family, friends, employers, and churches based on comments you left on social media platforms or voicing your opinion in other ways? Did you engage with others and add value to people who needed it? Did you convey more positive energy to energize others or more complaining that depleted your energy and that of others? Eleanor Roosevelt wrote in her book *You Learn by Living; Eleven Keys for a More Fulfilling Life*, "In the long run we shape our lives and we shape ourselves. The process never ends until we die. And the choices we make are ultimately our own responsibility." The choices we make are our thoughts, words, and actions. The choices we make are things we choose to do or choose not to do.

I never claimed this book would be magic, after reading it you would be perfect at having a positive mindset, all the time. Change is a process. You need continuous practice until it no long feels like work. Like me, you will have those moments that won't be your best self. Identify that moment, search why that happened, and prepare how to handle that differently next time. Acknowledge when you didn't do it well, but don't hold it against yourself. Learn from it. Be better next time. Don't forget to recognize when you did do it well. Celebrate that and then do it again. Surround yourself with those who will add value to you, who will hold you up when you're falling down, who will walk with you when things are rough, who won't judge you but will tell you the truth, and who will remind you that it's okay not to be okay but that you're loved. Remember to do the same for others.

When I see posts on social media where people ask for prayers or share something personal and people respond with praying hands and statements saying "praying," it makes me wonder, Do we post that and do it or do we simply post it? I've been more aware of my own responses, so if I say I'm praying, I pray right then and there. I want to be a person who has the highest integrity and does what she says she'll do. This is something I strive for each day—and I have really good days, some of the time. I want to surround myself with the type of people I described above, and I want others to choose me to be that person for them. What about you? *You get what you give* is a phrase I've heard so many times. Do you get what you give?

## PEZ Dispensers

As a child one of my favorite candies was PEZ and all the various dispensers. There are so many characters from which to choose! I've been using PEZ as an acronym for thirty years with my own twist:

**Passion.** A strong, intense, driving conviction; the commitment and desire about your ideas, your work, and your beliefs. We talk about having passion or knowing someone who's passionate about something or someone.

**Energy.** The positive motivation you use to express your ideas, accomplish your goals, and approach your daily tasks, situations, and people. It brings excitement, movement, and activity. We talk about being full of energy or depleted and drained. We get energized by other positive people.

**Zeal.** Eagerness, enthusiasm, fervor—an intensity of feeling or expression. It's a devotion to a cause, an idea, a goal, or a person. If you know a zealous person you can't help but be drawn to their energy and cause, usually because of their passion and energy.

Take time and figure out, Are you a PEZ Dispenser or someone who just eats all the candy? Be a PEZ Dispenser, and share your passion, energy, and zeal. Find ways to pour into others to build them up and, in turn, allow that to build you.

## SING YOUR SONG

I was singing in my car while driving to work. I was by myself, and it was one of my favorites. My car was transformed into my very own concert. I sang out loudly with passion. I usually lowered my voice when I stopped for a red light just in case anyone could hear me, even though my windows were up. This particular day I wasn't paying attention as I was stopped at a red light and I continued to sing, with my windows down. I looked to my right and there was a family. Staring at me. I stopped singing and smiled in embarrassment. The little girl said, "That was awesome!" Her smile warmed my heart. I'm not sure her parents agreed with her.

As I drove away, I thought about a time I was on a flight during a big storm. We were told to buckle up because we were going to experience some turbulence. Some turbulence. Some to me is a little bit. No, this was like being on a rollercoaster, which I don't like. We dipped down as my heart rose to my throat. We climbed back up and took a weird tilt to the right. The pilot got us stable. All the sudden from the back of the plane we heard little voices cheering and clapping, singing out, again, again! It made many of us laugh out loud. These little children thought it was a ride. They didn't see it as scary or known any reason to be worried.

This little girl didn't hear me like I did (or even as her parents probably did). She heard music and my passion. Hopefully, she knew I loved singing and what I was singing. When do we lose that type of innocence? We can learn a lot from children. They tell the truth, even when it might not be what we want to hear. As adults we tell them that's not nice. It may not be nice, but it's kind. The difference is we need to be kind and tell the truth and in how we deliver it. Let's not teach them to stop telling the truth; let's teach them how to tell the truth. As adults, we avoid telling others the truth, so we don't hurt their feelings, ruin a relationship, have conflict, get involved, etc. But not telling them the truth they probably need to hear is hurting them more. Children laugh at things we take too seriously. If we spent more time laughing, that builds into a more positive outlook and mindset. Children can hear and see beauty in others that we have tainted with our negative mindset and personal bias. They used to know how to engage with others without any issues, and now we wonder why adults need to take classes on how to build trust and relationships. They're fearless when it comes to doing things, taking chances we may not take as an adult.

Somewhere along the line we (the collective we) teach children to have a different, more negative mindset. We wonder why there's so much hate in this world; we've helped teach children negativity through our words, actions, and mindset. Children have a ton of energy, but when they sleep, they sleep. Adults have drink coffee and energy drinks and then cannot sleep unless they take a different pill. While children do need to learn from us so we can keep them safe and help them develop into self-functioning adults, we could learn a lot from children. Their minds are already *free*.

I still sing in my car. I sing at home. I'll forever sing, but not in front of others. And that is okay. I know my limitations and I know where my boundaries are for how I can express myself. It's when I'm singing, I'm my best self. When I need a pick-me-up, I can play a song and think of that little girl saying that was awesome. How about you? Are you ready to sing? Are you ready to be a PEZ Dispenser? I want to hear about your mindset shifts for a more positive outlook on how you have formulated your thoughts, reinvented yourself, engaged more positively with others, and how you energized yourself and others. Go, be awesome and sing your song. Sing it loud—I can't wait to hear it.

Go to **morethanyourmindset.com** to continue your learning journey with FREE resources.

# About the Author

**Karen Schumacher** understands what goes into being a business owner, volunteer, executive coach, and life coach, as well as a mom, wife, sister, daughter . . . Through one-on-one coaching, training workshops, and as a motivational speaker, she has inspired and empowered thousands of people to achieve their goals and work through obstacles holding them back. Karen has partnered with hundreds of companies across the United States for training, organizational, and leadership development and to create positive employment cultures. Her mission is simple: to grow others. She helps others turn their learning into action.

Made in the USA
Monee, IL
02 July 2022